Human Wrongs

British Social Policy and the
Universal Declaration of Human Rights

Human Wrongs

British Social Policy and the
Universal Declaration of Human Rights

T.J. Coles

BOOKS

Winchester, UK
Washington, USA

First published by iff Books, 2018
iff Books is an imprint of John Hunt Publishing Ltd., No. 3 East Street, Alresford,
Hampshire SO24 9EE, UK
office1@jhpbooks.net
www.johnhuntpublishing.com
www.iff-books.com

For distributor details and how to order please visit the 'Ordering' section on our website.

Text copyright: T.J. Coles 2017

ISBN: 978 1 78535 864 7
78 1 78535 865 4 (ebook)
Library of Congress Control Number: 2017953224

A CIP catalogue record for this book is available from the British Library.

Design: Stuart Davies

Printed and bound by CPI Group (UK) Ltd, Croydon, CR0 4YY, UK
US: Printed and bound by Edwards Brothers Malloy 15200 NBN Way #B, Blue Ridge Summit,
PA 17214, USA

We operate a distinctive and ethical publishing philosophy in
all areas of our business, from our global network of authors to
production and worldwide distribution.

Contents

Introduction

Preamble
...the advent of a world in which human beings shall enjoy freedom of speech and belief and freedom from fear and want has been proclaimed as the highest aspiration of the common people...

In 2018, the Universal Declaration of Human Rights (UDHR) will celebrate its 70th birthday. In principle, it is the most comprehensive set of rights and protections ever committed to paper. But in reality, it is only a piece of paper. Britain is legally bound to follow some of the articles of the UDHR; the ones absorbed into the legally-binding UN International Covenant on Civil and Political Rights (ICCPR) 1966, which Britain ratified in 1976. There is no enforcement mechanism for the UDHR, even within the ICCPR. The UDHR's main signatory and champion, Eleanor Roosevelt, explained at the time: the UDHR is 'not a treaty; it is not an international agreement. It is not and does not purport to be a statement of law or of legal obligation. It is a declaration of basic principles of human rights and freedoms to serve as a common standard of achievement for all peoples of all nations'.[1]

The UN explains that 'the UDHR has inspired a rich body of legally-binding international human rights treaties'. Notice that it does not say that the UDHR itself is legally binding; it is only binding through the ICCPR. Had an enforcement mechanism been included and had the UDHR been incorporated into domestic laws around the world, the declaration would have lifted millions out of oppression and abuses at the hands of their own nation-states, especially in those which strongly championed the UDHR: Britain and America.[2]

In celebration of its principles, if not its realization, this book analyzes the UK's domestic human rights and social justice record. It uses the 30 articles of the UDHR as a framework. Despite well-internalized propaganda which holds that Britain is one of the world's oldest democracies and remains a global beacon of liberty in terms of its judicial system and living standards, this book documents systematic violations of the UDHR by successive British governments. It may come as a surprise to many that on issue after issue, including child wellbeing, disability rights, union standards, the rights of demonstrators and freedom of speech, Britain has been repeatedly condemned by various agencies of the United Nations, as we shall see.[3]

It will come as no surprise that the government's response to the international criticisms has been denial, dismissal and contempt, with right-wing, privately-owned, mostly male-run media personally attacking many of the often female UN rapporteurs who raise concerns.[4]

THE DECLARATION

The UDHR was hardly a gift from elites. At the time of its adoption, two scholars in the *American Journal of International Law* (published much later in 1964) wrote: 'It is in response to the ever-increasing demands of people everywhere for greater access to, and wider sharing of, basic values,...that the United Nations program for human rights is being framed and implemented'. The UDHR itself makes clear in the preamble that it was adopted to safeguard elites: 'it is essential, if man is not to be compelled to have recourse, as a last resort, to rebellion against tyranny and oppression, that human rights should be protected by the rule of law'.[5]

Herbert Briggs writing at the time in the *American Journal of International Law* had a different opinion to Eleanor Roosevelt, who felt that the UDHR should be non-binding: 'The proposed Covenant on Human Rights (as it was then called) is intended to take the form of a treaty establishing binding obligations under international law'. Here begins a dichotomy: On the one hand, the Charter of the United Nations is legally binding for signatories, including the US and UK, and the UDHR is part of the charter; but on the other, the framers never intended it to be a legally binding document.[6]

The reasons appear to be that the policymakers of two of the world's leading human rights violators, Britain and America, did not want to subject themselves to laws that would see them tried for crimes against humanity. 'Congress barely noticed the UN General Assembly adoption of the Universal Declaration in 1948', writes Margaret E. Galey, echoing the situation in the UK, where almost nothing was said in Parliament about the UDHR in the first couple of decades following its adoption.[7]

The UDHR was immediately adopted by 48 nation-states. Eight abstained: the USSR (plus its allies and colonies), apartheid South Africa and Saudi Arabia; the latter two being close British allies. The UDHR emerged from the 18-member Commission on Human Rights. It was drafted by statesmen (few women, notably Eleanor Roosevelt,) and lawyers from the US, Britain, Canada and their allies.

In addition to the self-exemption standard (that is, making it a non-binding treaty), another self-serving contradiction emerges: the signing into law of the UDHR, which the leading framers assured the world was not law, was given very little media and scholarly attention, a fact that continues to the present. One of the most notable aspects of the UDHR is that it and its contents are concealed from the publics of signatory states by educational, media and cultural systems; all in violation of the UDHR itself, which states that governments should promote awareness about human rights.

Antoon De Baets of the University of Groningen laments the fact 'that historians have paid so little attention to the (UDHR)'. Likewise, Nebraska University's Professor David P. Forsythe notes that 'American political scientists seem not to have paid much attention to international human rights, for the most part'. In journals and symposia, '(o)ne searches in vain for more than brief recognition of international human rights developments'. Marjorie M. Whiteman was an advisor to Eleanor Roosevelt, who 'repeatedly asserted that the (UDHR) should be a "ringing declaration," to be committed to memory with ease and recited by school children the world over as we in America recite the opening clauses of our Declaration of Independence or the Preamble to the Constitution of the United States. In this, she was disappointed'.[8]

HOW BRITAIN RESPONDED

Charles Dukes, later Lord Dukeston (Labour), represented the UK as one of the nine Drafting Committee members, who worked between June 1946 and December 1948 to get the UDHR adopted (as GA resolution 217 A(III)). The British House of Lords says that the UDHR 'was the first international expression of universal standards on human rights'. According to the Lords, UDHR 'was created in order to provide a framework through which the aims of the United Nations (UN) Charter could be realised and protected'.[9]

According to the National Archives, the UDHR is important because it 'matters not only in times of conflict and in societies suffering repression, but also in addressing social injustice and achieving human dignity in times of peace in established democracies'. This book documents that this ideal has been actively opposed since the signing of the UDHR and remains ideologically opposed today.[10]

In a critique of the loss of rights under New Labour, future Tory MP Dominic Raab, writes that too much political leftism and selfishness has 'conflated' the so-called fundamental rights – liberty, presumption of innocence, freedom of speech, protection from arbitrary detention – with so-called wants: decent education, healthcare, decent housing and functioning public services. According to this view, the expansion of fundamental rights from abstractions, such as 'liberty', to concrete protections provided by the state, such as adequate housing, is an assault on rights. This kind of antihuman thinking is the core ideology of so-called New Conservatism. Raab blames the European Union and Britain's adoption of the Human Rights Act 1998 for the 'introduc(tion of) a socialist conception of human rights, fundamentally at odds with the British legacy of liberty'. Raab concludes that '(t)he result has been to upgrade endless ordinary claims, including to social services, NHS treatment, welfare payments and even police protection, to the status of fundamental human rights'.[11]

A lawyer, Raab conveniently omits Britain's obligation to the socialistic principles as codified in the ICCPR.

Naturally, the New Conservatives' view of the UDHR is at odds with the UDHR itself, but also with the National Archives' understanding of rights. Returning to the National Archives: 'Non-discrimination, equality and fairness, key components of justice, form the basis of the Declaration'. Like Raab, it also lauds the UK's supposed historical achievements. But unlike Raab, it states that these values translated into the UDHR and amount to progress, not regression. 'The ideas and values of human rights can be traced through history to ancient times and in religious beliefs and cultures around the world. In Britain', the National Archives continue, 'key developments include the Magna Carta of 1215, the Habeas Corpus Act of 1679 and the Bill of Rights of 1689'.[12]

The National Archives err, however, in claiming that UDHR 'has over time been accepted as a contract between governments and their peoples. Virtually all states have accepted it'. As this book documents, it is accepted only on paper; and even then, barely. 'The Declaration has also served as the foundation for an expanding system of human rights protection that today focuses also on vulnerable groups such as disabled persons, indigenous peoples and migrant workers'. Again, only on paper.[13]

Finally, the British Library describes the UDHR as 'the first global codification of rights to which all human beings are inherently entitled...British representatives' under the Labour government of the time 'were frustrated that it had moral but no legal obligation. It was not until 1976 that the International Covenant on Civil and Political Rights (ICCPR) came into force, giving a legal status to most of the UDHR'.[14]

Both the old Labour Party Constitution and the New Labour Constitution committed the party (and thus at times the government) to upholding United Nations principles. Clause IV article 7 of the old constitution committed Labour 'to support(ing) the United Nations and its various agencies and other international organisations for the promotion of peace, the adjustment and settlement of international disputes by conciliation or judicial arbitration, the establishment and defence of human rights, and the improvement of the social and economic standards and conditions of work of the people of the world'. The updated version reiterated Britain's formal commitment to UN principles. Clause IV article 3 states: 'Labour is committed to the defence and security of the British people, and to cooperating in European institutions, the United Nations, the Commonwealth and other international bodies to secure peace, freedom, democracy, economic security and environmental protection for all'. However, on social issues, New Labour erased its commitment to public ownership in the new constitution, and in doing so inadvertently rejected the UDHR and thus its commitments under the ICCPR.[15]

Both the Blair and Thatcher governments found terrorism-related excuses to derogate specific articles of the ICCPR. In Thatcher's day, it was Northern Irish terror. In Blair's, it was the 'war on terror'. Thatcher withdrew from articles 9, 9(3), 10 (2), 10 (3), 12 (1), 14, 17, 19 (2), 21 and 22. In order, these articles covered: arbitrary arrest and detention (thousands of

Irish were interned), bringing swift justice (many were held without charge), the segregation of convicts from suspects (including children), freedom of movement within one's own state (the British had every dwelling in Northern Ireland under surveillance), presumption of innocence, protection from arbitrary interference, freedom of expression (Northern Irish voices were banned from/distorted by national media), the right to peaceful assembly and the right to associate with others (including forming trade unions).[16]

Blair declared that following 9/11, a public emergency (Article 4(1)) justified abrogating Article 9 (protection from arbitrary arrest).[17]

WHAT SORT OF COUNTRY IS BRITAIN?

There are 65 million people living in the UK, about 9 million of whom were born abroad. Approximately 11.3 million families in the UK are in receipt of some kind of social security (e.g., child tax credit, housing benefits). The majority of claimants are in work and receiving benefits because levels of taxation are too high in relation to their incomes, as are living expenses. In addition, 8.7 million Britons receive a state pension. There are over 11 million disabled people in the UK, but only 3 million claim social security specifically for their disability. For over 9 million British families, social security accounts for half their income (or 30% of all British families). Despite propaganda citing the 'workshy' or Britain's supposed culture of entitlement and laziness, only 2% of households have a person who has never worked; half of whom are people between 18-25 years old. Fewer than 1% of welfare recipients engage in benefit fraud.[18]

Depending on the year and method of analysis, Britain is the fifth or sixth largest economy in the world, with a GDP of $2.8 trillion. Labour leader Jeremy Corbyn succeeded in making millions of Britons aware of this fact by including it in campaign speeches prior to the 2017 General Election, while Tory rival

Theresa May made every effort to conceal it. Despite this, 1 million Britons are dependent on food banks. This is due to a 'cash-flow problem', according to Tory MP Dominic Raab (the lawyer mentioned above), citing figures from the Trussell Trust, which runs food banks. Raab omitted that the trust explained that the 'cash-flow problem' is because people don't have enough money to live. Nearly one in three Britons (19.3 million) live in relative poverty (60% of whom are working families). Of these, 1 million are destitute: they are either homeless and/or have no money to keep clean, satiated or warm.[19]

Of the UK's 65 million residents, 134 are billionaires. Their combined wealth equals £658bn. The Office for National Statistics suggests that 10% of the population owns 44% of household wealth. One per cent owns 55% of the wealth. Britain has only two major political parties. The dominant Tory government receives over 50% of its funding from City of London Corporation-based financial institutions: asset managers, bankers, building societies, hedge funds, (re)insurers and liquidity firms. From the start of 2017 until the general election in the middle of the year, the Labour party received £8.1 million in small donations, after record numbers of people joined the party in an effort to ensure a socialist victory with Jeremy Corbyn as the leader. The Labour donations making up the £8.1m also came from unions and a few wealthier donors. In the same period, the Tories raised £15.2 million. As expected, Tory social policy reflects the interests of the wealthier donors: financial and business deregulation, tax breaks and cut backs on welfare instead of taxes on business. As the election drew closer, donations rose. In a single week, the Tories raised £3.77m compared to Labour's £331,499.[20]

The UN Economic and Social Council states: 'The adoption of fiscal consolidation programmes may be necessary for the implementation of economic and social rights.' Both Thatcherism, New Labourism and post-crash Tory-led austerity have dismantled such programmes. 'If such programmes are not implemented with full respect for human rights standards and do not take into account the obligations of States towards the rights holders', says the UN body (rights' holders meaning the public), 'they may adversely affect a range of rights protected by the International Covenant on Economic, Social and Cultural Rights', of which Britain is a signatory state and which contains many provisions of the UDHR. In contrast to the Raab view, the UN report concludes:

> Most at risk are labour rights, including the right to work (art. 6), the right to just and favourable conditions of work, including the right to fair wages and to a minimum wage that provides workers with a decent living for themselves and their families (art. 7), the right to collective bargaining (art. 8), the right to social security, including unemployment benefits, social assistance and old-age pensions (arts. 9 and 11), the right to an adequate standard of living, including the right to food and the right to housing (art. 11), the right to health and access to adequate health care (art. 12) and the right to education (arts. 13-14). Low-income families, especially those with children, and workers with the lowest qualifications are disproportionately affected by measures such as job cuts, minimum wage freezes and cutbacks in social assistance benefits, which potentially result in discrimination on the grounds of social origin or property.[21]

COMPARING CARING

In terms of social indicators, such as life expectancy, Britain compares poorly to other, comparably 'developed' nations. But it is worth noting that the post-Crash austerity is not the sole reason for Britain's social inequality. British society has long been dominated by intergenerational elites and *nouveau riche*, whose lobbying efforts, selfish ideologies and revolving-door business-to-politics *modus operandi* have had devastating effects on poorer members of society.

Writing in the 1980s, A.H. Halsey found that from the end of World War I to the 1970s, 'slow and steady progress' moved the UK 'towards a more equal distribution of personal income'. It is worth noting that the nascent Labour party, women's rights groups (mocked as suffragettes) and labour unions were instrumental in this push. By the 1970s, the top 10% held a quarter of the country's wealth; still uneven, but nothing as compared to today. Those on the bottom of the income scale also shared a quarter of the wealth. The rest was shared among the middle-classes.[22]

Due in large measure to nationalization and the creation of a welfare state by several Labour governments (those of Attlee and Wilson, who served twice), working class people entered the middle classes at the expense of the rich. The rich mobilized in the form of 'New Conservatism' or Thatcherism, in an effort to quickly regain their wealth. The Royal Commission on the Distribution of Income and Wealth found that between 1959 and 1975, the upper 1%'s wealth share 'declined continuously', from 8.4% to 6.2%. The upper 2-3%'s also 'declined'. The upper 10%'s share of the wealth fell from 29.4% to 26.6%. Between 1976 and 1982, with neoliberal economics underway, the bottom fifth lost literally half its wealth, down from the already meagre 0.8%, and the top regained its share.[23]

In 1980, the Western European average life expectancy across 13 countries, where figures are available, was 74.3 years (Iceland with 76.8 years was the highest, and Malta with 70.4 the lowest). By 2014, life expectancy across the same 11 countries averaged 82 years, with the UK below the average at 81.4 years (the lowest were Austria and Denmark at 80.7, the highest Spain and Switzerland at 83.3).[24]

In 1980, across 11 Western European countries where data are available, the average infant mortality rate per 1,000 births was 12.5 (Sweden had the lowest with 6.9 deaths per 1,000 births, Portugal had the highest with 24.3). The UK had above the Western European average, with 13.9 deaths per 1,000. In 2015, the average infant mortality across the same 11 countries had fallen to 2.6, thanks to education and more investment and advances in healthcare. The most impressive change was Portugal's, from 24.3 down to 2.9. To its shame, the UK lags behind Portugal in infant mortality, at 3.9: the second-to-worst in Western Europe, behind Malta and on a par with ex-Soviet Eastern European countries.[25]

Drawing on UN data, the KidsRights Index measures child wellbeing in terms of states' achievements versus their limitations. Somalia, for instance, gets a low score because it is not only one of the poorest countries in world, it has done virtually nothing for the rights of children since the Islamic Courts Union was overthrown in late-2006 by UK-backed proxy forces. Sweden, on the other hand, does well because it has the resources and it uses them. Britain does incredibly poorly because it has the resources but doesn't use them in the interests of its children, with regards to wellbeing, protection, integration, nutrition, family support and prospects.[26]

The 2017 index saw the UK plunge from 11th to 156th. At the top are Portugal, Norway, Switzerland, Iceland, Spain, France, Sweden, Thailand, Tunisia and Finland. At the bottom are the UK, Papua New Guinea, New Zealand, Guinea-Bissau, Equatorial Guinea, Chad, Vanuatu, Sierra Leone, Afghanistan and, in last place (of the countries surveyed), Central African Republic. The massive drop from 11th place to 156 was due to new analysing techniques which weigh a country's capability given its resources against its actual policies: in addition, data on state-civil cooperation was missing, unlike the previous years.[27]

Despite legislation to curb it, Britain is still ahead of Western European countries (except Belgium) when it comes to underage drinking: only Malta and Germany come close. Iceland, Portugal and France have the lowest levels. Despite record low numbers, by 2016 the UK still had the highest rate of underage pregnancy in Western Europe. The EU28 average is 6 births in every 1,000 by females aged 15 to 17. But this includes Eastern European countries. Britain is above the average at 6.8, above Estonia, Malta and Greece, but below Latvia, Hungary and Slovakia. Countries with the lowest rates are Sweden, Netherlands and Denmark.[28]

Britain also has some of the highest levels of sexual violence against women aged 18-29: Romania, Croatia and Poland have the lowest levels of reported abuse at 1.1%, 1.9% and 1.9% respectively, with France, the UK and Luxembourg having the highest: 12%, 12.3% and 13%. The UK is not even in the top ten global countries for human development in terms of life expectancy, income and education. The UN ranks it 16 at the time of writing, behind Lichtenstein (no. 15), Sweden, New Zealand, Hong Kong, the US, Canada, Iceland, Ireland, the Netherlands, Singapore, Denmark, Germany, Switzerland, Australia and Norway (no. 1).[29]

We turn now to the articles of the UDHR and document how successive British governments have violated them.

Chapter 1

Diego Garcia: free and equal?

Article 1

All human beings are born free and equal in dignity and rights. They are endowed with reason and conscience and should act towards one another in a spirit of brotherhood.

Britain's national status is Constitutional Monarchy and Parliamentary Democracy. Consequently, one may assume that British citizens are actually subjects of the crown, not 'free and equal' citizens. Part 1(1) of the British Nationality Act 1948, adopted in the year of the UDHR, states: 'Every person who under this Act is a citizen of the British United Kingdom and Colonies or...(has) the status of a British subject' for persons living in the Commonwealth. In other words, English, Welsh and Scots as former subjects were granted formal citizenship, but Irish and Commonwealth subjects remained subjects (until 1983, more below).[30]

All of this is irrelevant in a Constitutional Monarchy by virtue of an obscure veto the reigning monarch holds over legislation, known as the Royal Prerogative (also known as Crown Prerogative).[31]

Subsection 2 of the British Nationality Act 1948 states: 'the expression "British subject" and the expression "Commonwealth citizen" shall have the same meaning'. This is important for the people of Diego Garcia, which makes for a tragic test-case examined in this chapter, because future Acts granted them citizenship, yet the Royal Prerogative reduced them to the status of subjects. Her Majesty's Government website states that if one of numerous criteria were met, 'You became a British overseas territories citizen on 1 January 1983 if both of these apply (1) you were a citizen of the United Kingdom and Colonies on 31 December 1982 (2) you had connections with a British overseas territory because you, your parents or your grandparents were born, registered or naturalised in that British overseas territory'. This should apply to the people of Diego Garcia.[32]

A HISTORY OF THE ISLANDS

Diego Garcians were known as Ilois, French Creole for 'islanders', now as Chagossians. They inhabited the island from the late-eighteenth century to the early-1970s, when they were expelled by the British military. The Chagossians came from slaves, plantation workers and managers. During the nineteenth century, they developed a unique democratic culture. 'No one was involuntarily unemployed. Most of the Chagossians were illiterate and their skills were confined to those needed for the activities on the islands. But they had a rich community life', the House of Lords concedes. '(T)he Roman Catholic religion and their own distinctive dialect derived (like those of Mauritius and the Seychelles) from the French. Into this innocent world there intruded, in the 1960s, the brutal realities of global politics'.[33]

The Chagos Archipelago lies south of the equator in the Indian Ocean. Its largest island, Diego Garcia, was ceded to Britain by France with the Treaty of Paris 1814, after the Napoleonic Wars. Its formal status was a Dependency of Mauritius, the latter being a British crown colony, also taken from France. Diego Garcia's unique position protects islanders from floods, hurricanes and earthquakes, making it an ideal site for military operations, hence the establishment of a Royal Air Force base on the island in the Second World War.[34]

In 1965, Britain created the British Indian Ocean Territory (BIOT), Diego Garcia being the main island in the territory. The purpose was to regain control of Diego Garcia after Mauritius was decolonized so that the United States, under a 50-year lease, renewable in 20-year periods, could use it as a military base. The excision of Diego Garcia from Mauritius through the Lancaster House Agreement, a violation of UN laws on decolonization and an issue still disputed with Mauritius, was formalized by an Order in Council; a monarchic legal ritual in which government appointees read legislation to the monarch, who approves or rejects the given order. The Lords confirm that 'by an exception in the Mauritius Independence Act 1968, (the Chagossians) did not lose their UK citizenship'.[35]

Legal specialist Maureen Tong writes: 'The UN General Assembly Resolution 2066 (XX) of 16 December 1965 prohibited the dismemberment of Mauritius to establish the US military base in Diego Garcia'. She continues: 'The excision of the Chagos archipelago to establish the BIOT in 1965 contravened Resolution 1514 (XV)'. The original Order in Council establishing Diego Garcia as British Indian Ocean Territory was arguably the first royal act that sought to deprive the Chagossians of their rights. It demonstrates that in a monarchy, citizens are indeed subjects. It is also worth noting that as part of the 1966 agreement with the US, Britain received a £14 million reduction in its sea-based Polaris nuclear system, which it purchased from America.[36]

From 1968 to 1973, the islanders were forcibly removed by the British military and deported to the slums of the Seychelles, Mauritius and London, where they have remained ever since. Depopulation was necessitated by UN regulations regarding decolonization. It would have been contrary to international law for the US to take over a populated territory (colonialism), so the solution was to depopulate Diego Garcia. Britain's act of forcible exile prevented the US from being scrutinized by the UN Special Committee on the Situation with Regard to the Implementation of the Declaration on the Granting of Independence to Colonial Countries and Peoples.[37]

GETTING THE PEOPLE OFF
The British Colonial Office made this perfectly clear in secret,

internal records. For the colonial officials:

> to recognise that there are any permanent inhabitants will imply that there is a population whose democratic rights will have to be safeguarded and which will therefore be deemed by the UN to come within its purlieu. The solution proposed is to issue them with documents making it clear that they are 'belongers' of Mauritius and the Seychelles and only temporary residents of BIOT. This device, although rather transparent, would at least give us a defensible position to take up (at the UN).[38]

Denis (later Lord) Greenhill, head of the Colonial Office, explained the UK's position in a memorandum to the British Delegation at the UN: 'The object of the exercise is to get some rocks which will remain ours; there will be no indigenous population except seagulls who have not yet got a committee. Unfortunately, along with the seagulls go some few (sic) Tarzans and Men Fridays that are hopefully being wished on Mauritius'.[39]

When Members of Parliament began asking questions, the Foreign Office strategy was to administer briefing papers to MPs concerning Diego Garcia. Eleanor Emery, head of the Foreign Office's Indian Ocean department, outlined the strategy in a secret paper: 'We would not wish it to become general knowledge that some of the inhabitants have lived on Diego Garcia for several generations and could, therefore, be regarded as "belongers"'. She went on to say that: 'We shall advise ministers in handling supplementary questions to say that there is only a small number of contract workers from the Seychelles and Mauritius, engaged to work on the copra plantations'.[40]

In 1967, the British Commissioner declared an Acquisition of Land for Public Purposes (Private Treaty) Ordinance, preventing the Chagos Agalega Company from operating on the islands. This meant that temporary workers had to leave, draining the economy with the possible intended effect of impelling the indigenous islanders to leave. This was phase two of the expulsion preparations. Phase three was the issuance of an Immigration Ordinance to clear the island of its inhabitants. In another secret memo, the Foreign and Commonwealth Office explained: 'The purpose of the Immigration Ordinance is to maintain the fiction that the inhabitants of the Chagos (sic) are not a permanent or semi-permanent population'. These were secret admissions that the population had a right to stay.[41]

Phase one of the physical expulsion of approximately 1,700 Chagossians began in 1969, when the working contracts were terminated. This left those working in Mauritius stranded. When relatives travelled to Mauritius to assist their families, they too became stranded. As for phase two, 'British officials began restricting supplies to the islands and more Chagossians left as food and medicines dwindled...UK officials forced the remaining islanders to board overcrowded cargo ships and left them on the docks in Mauritius and the Seychelles'. David Vine's Princeton University-published study continues: 'Just before the last deportations, British agents and US troops on Diego Garcia herded the Chagossians' pet dogs into sealed sheds and gassed and burned them in front of their traumatized owners awaiting deportation'. Survivor and exile Rita Bancoult, who has suffered further personal tragedies in the slums of Mauritius, says: 'It's as if I was pulled from my paradise to put me in hell. Everything here you need to buy. I don't have the means to buy them. My children go without eating. How am I supposed to bear this life?'.[42]

Rita's son, Olivier, formed the Chagos Refugees Group. Olivier and others continued to struggle for repatriation, becoming official citizens in 1981. In 2000, Olivier brought a case against the Secretary of State for Foreign and Commonwealth Affairs (Robin Cook) to the High Court.

THE RIGHT OF RETURN?

The High Court granted the islanders the right to return to Diego Garcia. They had not the means to return and legislated for compensation in 2004. In June of that year, Elizabeth II overruled the High Court decision with two Orders in Council, banning the islanders from their home in perpetuity. One of the Orders was the British Indian Ocean Territory (Constitution) Order 2004, which states: 'no person has the right of abode in the Territory'.[43]

In May 2006, the High Court declared the government's decision unlawful, stating: 'The suggestion that a minister can, through the means of an order in council, exile a whole population from a British overseas territory and claim that he is doing so for the 'peace, order and good government' of the territory is, to us, repugnant'.[44]

The Court of Appeal dismissed the government's 2007 action against the High Court. In 2008, the Government brought the matter to the Appellate Committee House of Lords, which overturned the High Court's ruling by a judgement of three to two: Lords Carwell, Hoffman and Rodger voting in the government's favour, that the Royal Prerogative was appropriate. This tells us much about the nature of British democracy, particularly that the Lords can overrule High Court decisions and that the monarch has 'full power to establish such executive, legislative, and judicial arrangements as this Crown thinks fit', particularly in relation to colonies, to quote Halsbury's *Laws of England*. It also tells us that citizens have official status, but are in reality subjects.[45]

In 2009, the British government sought to make the BIOT a 'marine nature reserve', with exceptions for US military purposes. A leaked memo written by Political Counsel Richard Mills states: 'the BIOT's former inhabitants would find it difficult, if not impossible, to pursue their claim for resettlement on the islands if the entire Chagos Archipelago were a marine reserve'. Mills quotes and paraphrases Colin Roberts, the FCO's Commission of the BIOT: '"there are proposals (for a marine park) that could provide the Chagossians warden jobs" within the BIOT. However, Roberts stated that, according to the HGM's current thinking on a reserve, there would be "no human footprints" or "Man Fridays" on the BIOT's uninhabited islands', note the same language and attitude 50 years on. 'He asserted that establishing a marine park would, in effect, put paid to resettlement claims of the archipelago's former residents...(Roberts said) "We do not regret the removal of the population"'.[46]

In 2015, Mauritius took Britain to the International Court of Justice over its obligation, agreed in 1965, to decolonize the Chagos archipelago, including Diego Garcia. Mauritius's specific complaint was that the UK had illegally drawn a Marine Protection Area (MPA) in 2010, restricting operations (including fishing) around the British Indian Ocean Territory. The Permanent Council for Arbitration ruled 'that the creation of the MPA violated international law'. The UK has ignored the ruling and the islanders are left to wonder where the decision puts them, legally speaking.[47]

The Chagossians continue their struggle and can be assisted in Britain via the UK Chagos Support Association. Let us now turn to the British mainland.

Chapter 2

...without distinction

Article 2

Everyone is entitled to all the rights and freedoms set forth in this Declaration, without distinction of any kind, such as race, colour, sex, language, religion, political or other opinion, national or social origin, property, birth or other status. Furthermore, no distinction shall be made on the basis of the political, jurisdictional or international status of the country or territory to which a person belongs, whether it be independent, trust, non-self-governing or under any other limitation of sovereignty.

Most of this book concerns poor people because they are the ones disproportionately affected by government policy. In addition to poor people, middle-class women, ethnic minorities and people with so-called disabilities face institutional and socioeconomic discrimination, in violation of Article 2 of the UDHR.

ETHNIC INEQUALITIES

Many factors coincide to put British ethnic minorities at the bottom of the scale when it comes to socioeconomic indicators, in most cases. In times of economic downturn, ethnic minorities are often more at risk than whites.

The recession in the 1990s resulted in a 10% rise in unemployment among blacks compared to 6% among whites. Most of us are familiar with Brexit-related attacks on minorities after the Referendum result in June 2016, but this is nothing new. At the dawn of the millennium, a United Nations Committee on the Elimination of Racial Discrimination criticized the high level of racially-motivated attacks in the UK, institutional racism in the police and 'high unemployment and school exclusion rates among ethnic minorities'.[48]

The financial crisis 2008 and its aftermath made things worse. The crisis and the government's handling of it left 50% of black people aged 16-25 unemployed, compared with 20% of whites. The Department for Work and Pensions puts the figure of Asian unemployment for 16-24-year-olds at 46%. According to the House of Commons Library, by 2015, there were 41,000 16-to-24-year-old black, Asian and other ethnic minorities 'long-term unemployed – a 49% rise from 2010'.[49]

Dr Laurence Brown of Manchester University's Centre on Dynamics of Ethnicity says that 'ethnic minorities in Britain are, in many cases, outperforming their white peers in both secondary and higher education. However, very few of these gains in education have translated into employment outcomes'. One third of ethnic Bangladeshis and Pakistanis in England and a fifth of Arabs, Black Africans and Black Caribbeans, live in the most deprived areas, compared to one tenth of white Britons. Black African and Caribbean women experienced a 15-20% decline in full-time employment between 2004 and 2014, compared to relative stability for white women. Among Bangladeshi women, 39% have experienced a doubling of part-time work over the last 20 years.[50]

Around the time of Brexit, with pro-'nationalist' spokespeople like Nigel Farage given airtime and press coverage, many racists and xenophobes who would not have otherwise acted on their prejudices felt vindicated by the 'Leave' result and started attacking both migrants and Britons from ethnic minorities. The UN Committee on the Elimination of Racial Discrimination stated: 'Many politicians and prominent political figures not only failed to condemn it but also created and entrenched prejudices, thereby emboldening individuals to carry out acts of intimidation and hate towards ethnic or ethno-religious minority communities and people who are visibly different'.[51]

The government's Casey Report (2012) reviewed a decade

of community cohesion and race relations. It concluded that successive governments had failed to implement advice from communities:

> But the awareness of many of these issues and subsequent failures to address them arguably makes the situation worse, not better. The problem has not been a lack of knowledge but a failure of collective, consistent and persistent will to do something about it or give it the priority it deserves at both a national and local level. The work that has been done has often been piecemeal and lacked a clear evidence base or programme of evaluation.[52]

GENDER INEQUALITY

In 2008, towards the end of the New Labour government, a committee of the UN's Convention on the Elimination of All Forms of Discrimination Against Women found that 'British women are under-represented in Parliament, paid less than men at work and increasingly being sent to prison for committing minor offences'. It concluded that women's pay was on average 17% lower than men's.[53]

A couple of years later, 40 years after the introduction of the Equal Pay Act 1970, the Chartered Management Institute found that women will not be paid as much as men until 2067, at the rate of current trends. Britain ranked 18 in the Global Gender Gap Report 2014. A year later, Britain's position had slipped to 26, indicating the fragility of women's position in society.[54]

According to FTSE 100 data, 93% of modern corporations are run by men. Opportunity Now surveyed 25,000 women. 'Almost a fifth of the women surveyed so far say that their careers have stalled because managers failed to promote them or offer training opportunities'. Forty-eight per cent said they had been bullied or witnessed gender-based bullying, compared to 28% of men. A House of Commons Library report 2012 finds that 'unemployment among women aged 50 to 64 has risen by 39% in the (since 2010), compared with an overall rise of 5% among over-16s' — partly due to age discrimination. The Fawcett Society estimates 'the actual percentage of women at risk from public sector cuts to be (close to) 70 per cent, while the Chartered Institute of Personnel and Development puts that figure at closer to 80 per cent'.[55]

In 2014, legal scholar Dr Rashida Manjoo, Special Rapporteur for the UN Human Rights Council, criticized Britain's 'boys' club, sexist culture'. Dr Manjoo described a culture of impunity, in which women are sexualized and 'marketis(ed)'. Sexual bullying and harassment is 'routine' and austerity has a 'disproportionate' effect on women, many of whom suffer the ire of their dejected partners. Dr Manjoo was denied a visit to the Yarl's Wood 'facility', where women and girls facing deportation are held, many of whom for indefinite periods.[56]

By 2015, Britain ranked 27th out of 36 OECD countries for the percentage of its female politicians (22.70%), falling behind commensurate countries such as Germany (33.30%) and France (50%), as well as Chile (34.80%), Colombia (29.40%) and Latvia (23.1%).[57]

DISABLING THE DISABLED

In 2014, the UK received the dubious honour being the first country to be investigated by the UN Committee on the Rights of Persons with Disabilities for what campaigners call 'grave violations' of human rights, particularly relating to Department for Work and Pensions' social security cuts (or 'war on benefits', as an article interviewing then-Minister Iain Duncan Smith called it). In a separate instance, Raquel Rolnik, the UN Special Rapporteur for Housing, condemned the Under Occupancy Charge, or 'Bedroom Tax', as breaching the human rights of disabled persons by making the extra rooms in their accommodation unaffordable. Rolnik then faced a torrent of personal abuse from the press.[58]

Nearly a decade earlier, under New Labour (3 years before the financial crisis), the Joseph Rowntree Foundation found that although income poverty had fallen for the general population to 1987 levels, it had *risen* for the disabled. In 2005, 30% of disabled adults lived in poverty, a higher percentage than under the Tories in 1995 and double the average for non-disabled persons. 'Around 800,000 disabled people aged between 25 and retirement age are (classed as) 'economically inactive, but wanting work'', compared with 200,000 non-disabled persons.[59]

By the end of the New Labour regime, little had changed. 'In England, 17% of children with Special Educational Needs (SEN) got five good GCSEs including English and Maths, compared to 61% of children without identified SEN', according to a report by the Equality and Human Rights Commission (2010). 'This does not just apply to people with learning disabilities: only 33% of children whose primary need related to visual impairment attained this level...Of children with SEN and who are eligible for (free school meals), only 10% of girls and 8% of boys in England obtain 5 good GCSEs including English and Maths'. The report also notes that '(a)cross Britain, disabled adults are three times as likely as others to have no qualifications'.[60]

According to law firm Leigh Day and Co., by 2014, 7 million disabled persons were employed in the UK, but only 4 million were protected by the Equality Act 2010. Despite numerous Disability Discrimination Acts being introduced, one in five face discrimination at work, 47% of disabled persons would not feel confident about disclosing their disabilities and 20% of current employed feel unsupported by colleagues and bosses. At the time of the study, 334,000 disabled persons worked in environments not adapted for their needs. Of the 44% who asked for adjustments, 31% saw no or few adjustments made. 'Those with higher educational attainment (degree/post graduate) are more likely to have asked for workplace adjustments ... than those with medium level education', which is difficult given the limitations on education for disabled persons.[61]

In 2014, Oxford-educated Department for Work and Pensions welfare minister, Lord Freud, said that the disabled are 'not worth the full wage' and could be paid £2 an hour.[62]

Chapter 3

Killing them softly

Article 3
Everyone has the right to life, liberty and security of person.

At the time of writing, 80 people are known to have died in the Grenfell Tower tragedy, Kensington and Chelsea, London. Kensington-Chelsea is the richest borough in London and one of the wealthiest places in the world. But it also hosts pesky poor people crammed into slums. In 2017, a fire spread throughout the tower due in large part to absent health, safety and fire-prevention materials, such as sprinklers. The tower bloc had previously been clad with flammable materials in order to hide it, and the poor, thereby not disturbing the aesthetic enjoyment of the borough's wealthier occupants.[63]

The event was a wake-up call to the growing class and wealth divisions in the UK. The surviving tenants had not been rehoused in nearby council homes and some of them had even been charged for rent *after* the fire. The public, not the incumbent May government, expressed an outpouring of grief. But where is the outpouring of grief for the families burned to death and blown to pieces by RAF bombers in Iraq, Libya and Syria? Sticking to the UK, where is the outpouring of grief for the 40,000 Britons, most of them poor and living in poor areas, who die from pollution-rated diseases every year?[64]

This chapter examines the silent victims of British economic violence.

EUTHANASIA: 'REDUCING THE BURDEN OF CARE'
One particular demographic denied the right to life is the elderly

poor. In a projection to 2036 anticipating social trends, the UK Ministry of Defence writes: 'Declining youth populations in Western societies could become increasingly dissatisfied with their economically burdensome 'baby-boomer' elders, among whom much of societies' wealth would be concentrated'. It goes on to say: 'Resentful at a generation whose values appear to be out of step with tightening resource constraints, the young might seek a return to an order provided by more conservative values and structures'. In conclusion, the MoD writes: 'This could lead to a civic renaissance, with strict penalties for those failing to fulfil their social obligations. It might also open the way to policies which permit euthanasia as a means to reduce the burden of care for the elderly'.[65]

In 2012, making no reference to the above document, the BBC revealed that for many years a silent geronticide has been carried out within the increasingly-privatized National Health Service. Although the NHS is well-funded, much of the funding goes to paying private service providers, debts incurred by privatization and into the pockets of corrupt trusts, which manage hospitals. The NHS has been operating a nationwide system called the Liverpool Care Pathway (LCP). A BBC television report described the system as denying food, water, and medicine to terminally ill, elderly patients for their own benefit (some seniors become too senile to swallow, for instance,) and 'to free up beds'.[66]

But families have complained that elderly relatives were put on the LCP and died, whereas many would have survived. One victim who merely contracted a chest infection was the mother of high-profile TV chef Rustie Lee. She survived because Lee found her in time.[67]

According to the *Daily Mail*, 450,000 die each year in NHS hospitals, 130,000 of whom are LCP patients. It is estimated that 60,000 individuals die prematurely each year as a result of LCP. When the LCP system was recommended for hospitals in 2004, University of London Professor Emeritus Peter Millard and

Dr Peter Hargreaves, a palliative care consultant at St Luke's, cautioned against 'backdoor euthanasia'. In a lecture to the Royal Society of Medicine, neurology specialist Professor Patrick Pullicino said: 'The lack of evidence for initiating (LCP) makes it an assisted death pathway rather than a care pathway. Very likely many elderly patients who could live substantially longer are being killed'. He adds: 'Patients are frequently put on the pathway without a proper analysis of their condition'.[68]

It should be noted that many terminally-ill patients want to die and should be assisted in their deaths, but many do not and are quietly murdered. Unless their inheritance can be taxed or some insurance payoffs given, the terminally ill serve no economic function and are a hindrance to the contemporary health market. Robert Goold (aged 69) was admitted to hospital suffering from dementia. He was put on LCP without his family's knowledge or consent. He spent eight days without food or water. 'You wouldn't treat a dog the way my poor dad was treated', said his daughter, Susan Phillips. 'We are all devastated, the best interests of the patient was not starving him to death'.[69]

The *Telegraph* reports that 'the NHS was accused of handing out a £30 million "bribe" to hospitals who hit targets for the number of patients who die on the LCP' after a 'tide of horror stories from patients' families about the programme being arbitrarily imposed on their loved ones' was revealed.[70]

Temperature is another pensioner-killer.

'EXCESS WINTER DEATHS'

As government-subsidized energy giants continued to post record profits, the Office for National Statistics reported that around 31,100 'excess winter deaths occurred in England and Wales in 2012/13 – a 29% increase compared with the previous winter'. The right-wing *Spectator* writes: 'The UK rates for 'excess winter mortality' ought to be seen as a national scandal: they are almost twice that of far-colder Norway'. It cites a study in the *British Medical Journal* (*BMJ*) analysing data from 1998-2000. The *BMJ*-published study notes that countries with colder winter climates, including Finland, 'appear to suffer far less from excess winter mortality'. The paper cites home insulation as a key factor. 'Exemplary levels of thermal efficiency are found in Scandinavian countries(,) Sweden, Norway, and Finland'.[71]

Chris Huhne, then-Secretary of State for Energy and Climate Change, stated: 'Britain has some of the oldest building stock in Europe. Our draughty homes are poorly insulated, leaking heat and using up energy. As consumers, we pay a high price for inefficient housing – and so does the planet'. The Tory-Liberal coalition's solution was to offer loans to customers under a Green Deal, the professed aim of which was to comply with Britain's carbon emission requirements. A Parliamentary Committee on the scheme concluded that 'high interest rates on loans (were) widely regarded as unattractive, (with) ministers forced to admit that savings' on energy bills, made with thermal insulation, 'were not guaranteed' (*Telegraph*). Of the 1 million homes supposed to benefit from the scheme, 'Fewer than 4,000 households had signed up for 'Green Deals' by the end of July (2013)'.[72]

Chapter 4

Slavery and servitude…in all their forms

Article 4

No one shall be held in slavery or servitude; slavery and the slave trade shall be prohibited in all their forms.

Forced/coerced labour, slavery, not only exists in UK prisons for the benefit of corporations (not in the public interest as some legislation permits), it also exists in the supply-chains of some major UK-based corporations. The Justice and Coroners Act 2003 contained vague provisions against servitude. It was as late as the Modern Slavery Act 2015 that Britain finally, explicitly legislated against slavery in the UK. The Act says nothing about state-slavery in prisons and lets big business off the hook, as ethics group CORE explains: 'The draft Bill contained no mention of company supply chains, despite recommendations from the evidence review and the Bill committee that a requirement on businesses to make their supply chains more transparent be included in the legislation'.[73]

SLAVERY IN SUPPLY CHAINS

A whole third of the world's poor are concentrated in India and, not surprisingly, there is a correlation with slavery. The Global Slavery Index (2014) notes that, 'In terms of absolute numbers, India remains top of the list with an estimated 14.29 million enslaved people', making up about 40% of the world's slave population. India is 'followed by China (3.24m), Pakistan (2.06m), Uzbekistan (1.2m…), and Russia (1.05m)'.[74]

Most of India's slaves are bonded labourers, meaning that they or their families owe debts which they have to work to pay off. The majority also happen to be Dalits, people at the bottom of India's racist caste system. About 240 million Indian children work. 60 million of those are hard labourers and some 10 million are outright slaves. A BBC investigation in September 2015 found child labourers working on tea plantations owned by the company McLeod Russell, which supplies tea for Liptons, PG Tips, Tetleys and Twinings. The companies deny all knowledge and responsibility and claim that they are acting to stop or have stopped employees using slaves.[75]

In 2015, a *Guardian* investigation revealed that the UN, the Asian Development Bank and the UK's Department for International Development had funded hotel and airport construction projects in Nepal that utilized bonded labour, including 28,000 Nepalese children, half of whom are under 14 years old. Turning to Bangladesh, an ITV investigation revealed that girls as young as 13 were working for up to 11 hours in padlocked factories in Dhaka owned by Vase Apparels making garments for British-based firms, including Southbay menswear and Lee Cooper jeans. The products, many supplied by the Fielding Group, were found in ASDA (owned by Wal-Mart), BHS (then owned by Arcadia Group), JD Williams (owned by N Brown), Premier Man and Jacamo. The companies again deny knowledge and responsibility, claiming that they will root out slavery in supply chains.[76]

SLAVERY IN UK PRISONS

The Slavery Convention 1926 permits criminal penal labour in the public interest. What the ex-convict-founded Campaign Against Prison Slavery (CAPS) discovered, however, is that British prisoners are frequently coerced into labouring for private corporations.

Disproportionate numbers of prisoners (valued against the non-prison population) come from broken homes, foster families, are runaways, dyslexics, poorly educated, have addictions and/ or mental illnesses and are from ethnic minorities. There is nothing wrong with prison workshops. They can be used to educate prisoners, give them the self-esteem missing outside of prison, and prepare them for work. In the real world, however, most employers refuse to employ former convicts. Most prisoners have no jobs to go to upon leaving prison. Ergo, prison workshops become exploitation centres. Prisoners are a perfect captive population for corporate and state exploitation. CAPS, now defunct, found modern slavery in 100 UK prisons. Here are some examples of the prisons and what the inmates are forced to pack, produce, paint, print, cut and sew (since the report some prisons have closed for unrelated reasons):[77]

HMP Acklington (extension cables), Belmarsh (halogen lights, brass pins for power sockets), Camp Hill (light stands, caravan steps and ladders), Dartmoor (pixie and gnome painting, fibre optic joiners), Exeter (plumbing parts, packing and assembling tractor parts), Full Sutton (assembling contact lens cleaning fluid containers), Guys Marsh Louvered (potpourri, fragrance oils), Haverigg (stationery and garden plant furniture), Kingston (light fittings and cat's eyes), Littlehey (arcade machine components, wooden fences), Morton Hall (lampshades, greeting cards), Nottingham Battery (coat hangers, plastic wallets), Parkhurst (bicycles), Ranby (electrical toothbrushes), Springhill and Grendon (camera bags and battery packing), Verne (lobster pot assembly, TV repair), and Wealstun (drinks, vegetable and mushroom packing).[78]

According to CAPS, there were 4,700 prisoners in Contract Services workshops by 2008, generating £6.1 million for the prison service. Under the New Labour government (1997-2010), the prison population doubled, providing an abundance of captive labour. 'Clothing and textiles is the biggest employer in prison workshops with roughly 3,000 prisoners involved across 60 prisons', says CAPS. The organization provides an example of how coerced labour is extracted: 'One correspondent has told of how, within 1 year of his release, he refused to fold pieces of paper for mail shots 7.5 hours a day, 5 days a week "because he found it degrading and an insult to the prisoners' intelligence". His stand resulted in a move back to closed conditions and ultimately cost him 2 years on his sentence'.[79]

Chapter 5

Torture and degrading treatment

Article 5

No one shall be subjected to torture or to cruel, inhuman or degrading treatment or punishment.

Britain has a long history of torturing colonial subjects, including burning Kenyan civilians to death as late as the 1950s. In '70s Northern Ireland, torture was routine as part of the hostage-taking known as internment. Today, British forces torture civilians abroad and train and arm those, like the Iraqi police and the Rapid Action Battalion of Bangladesh, who also torture. As part of the so-called 'war on terror', Britain allowed its Diego Garcia territory, which, as noted, hosts a US military base, to be used as a 'rendition' site for the kidnap and torture of civilians. The mainland has also been used for US planes carrying kidnapped suspects on their way to be tortured in other countries.[80]

In the case of Diego Garcia, the Blair government stated: 'The Convention Against Torture does not apply on Diego Garcia', that is, on British territory. The government was able to get away with this due to the invocation of the Royal Prerogative mentioned in Chapter 1.[81]

Martin Scheinin was the UN Special Rapporteur on the Promotion and Protection of Human Rights and Fundamental Freedoms While Countering Terrorism. His 2009 report names several countries, including the UK, as helping the US rendition programme. 'While this system was devised and put in place by the United States, it was only possible through collaboration from many other States'. The report concludes: 'States...are responsible where they knowingly engage in, render aid to or assist in the commission of internationally wrongful acts, including violations of human rights'.[82]

The cases of Diego Garcia and Northern Ireland show that Britain tortures in its own supposed territories. The UN Committee Against Torture's report on the UK (2013) expressed concern about the British Tory government's 'position on the extraterritorial application of the Convention (Against Torture), in particular that although its armed forces are required to comply with the absolute prohibition against torture as set out in the Convention, it considers that the scope of each article of the Convention "must be considered on its terms"', meaning the government permits torture at will. But what about on the British mainland?[83]

One widespread form of torture, which the public and intelligentsia do not even seem to realize is torture, is the use of electroshock weapons. The police in England and Wales regularly use weapons against the British public, including those which the UN has condemned as torture weapons. In 2007, the United Nations Committee Against Torture found that 'the use of TaserX26 weapons, provoking extreme pain, constituted a form of torture'. These weapons were rolled out to previously unarmed police beginning in 2003 under Tony Blair's New Labour government. Two probes hit the victim and deliver up to 50,000-volt shocks.[84]

By mid-2016, 16 individuals had died as a result of taser-related policing; some had been shot by armed police prior to being tasered (which defeats the alleged point of tasering), others shot or cut themselves. Between 2004 and 2013, taser usage increased by 232%. To date, two blind men (one aged 61, the other aged 43) on separate occasions were tasered by police who claimed to have mistaken their white canes for swords. Andrew Pimlott was burned to death by police who fired a taser at him when he doused himself in petrol. Adrian Thompson died after being tasered by police who claimed that he was burgling a house, when in fact he was an invited party guest. In an infamous case, former Aston Villa football star Dalian Atkinson died after being tasered three times.[85]

Two-thirds of taser victims have a mental illness, according to the Home Office.[86]

Between January 2014 and November 2015, 407 children, some as young as 12, were tasered by police. The London Metropolitan Police Service alone tasered 185 children in the same period. Once again, class is an issue: few victims are middle- or upper-class.[87]

MENTAL TORTURE

British children and youths are also subjected to psychological torture.

In so-called young offender institutions (or child prisons), one in three are put into isolation cells. The Criminal Justice Act 1982 replaced borstals with youth detention centres and resulted in what some judges and ministers called the 'short, sharp shock' treatment. In 1985, during Thatcher's reign, cutbacks to services resulted in '(s)taff (being) so stretched that (young) inmates were now regularly locked up for 23 hours a day, and control problems were rapidly reaching crisis proportions', to quote media reports from the period.[88]

Little has changed. A 2015 report by the Children's Commission found that a third of all children in prison end up in isolation, some for up to 22-23 hours per day. 'Black/mixed heritage and looked after children (are) more likely to experience isolation' than white children from so-called non-broken homes. Children's Commissioner Anne Longfield says: 'The practice of segregating children for 22 hours or more per day should stop. Even where there are children who may never be released from prison long periods of segregation is likely to have detrimental effect on their behaviour and outcomes' (sic). In addition to violent behaviour, some children 'are locked up (in isolation) because of staff shortages, while others elect to be isolated to give them 'time out' from groups'.[89]

Chapter 6

It's cheaper to plead guilty

Article 6

Everyone has the right to recognition everywhere as a person before the law.

As noted in Chapter 1, Britons are both citizens (on paper) and subjects (*de facto*). The queen's invocation of the Royal Prerogative to overturn the High Court decision of 2002 (regarding the people of Diego Garcia) exemplifies the arbitrary nature of individual rights in the UK.

Legal aid is government sponsorship for poor plaintiffs and defendants. Cuts imposed stringent criteria on the service, meaning that for civil issues, like disabled people taking legal action against the government for cutting their benefits, individuals are no longer entitled to funding. The UN Economic and Social Council (2016) writes about the cuts: 'The Committee is concerned that the reforms to the legal aid system and the introduction of employment tribunal fees have restricted access to justice in areas such as employment, housing, education and social welfare benefits'.[90]

Historian Barry Reay notes of eighteenth-century England: '(e)ven though the costs of prosecuting a misdemeanour were cheaper for felonies', for the poor 'they were still a disincentive... It was cheaper to plead guilty'. How much has changed in three centuries? In 2015, the *Guardian* reported: 'Magistrates have begun to resign in protest at punitive court charges of up to £1,200 that they claim can never be collected and encourage the innocent to plead guilty'. Richard Monkhouse, chair of the Magistrates Association, says: 'Our members have expressed concerns about the charge from the outset and it shows the strength of feeling when experienced magistrates resign from the bench because of it'.[91]

The New Labour government failed to raise legal aid. After four years of a Liberal-Tory coalition, the service was cut by nearly 9%. In 2012, the coalition introduced the Legal Aid, Sentencing and Punishment of Offenders Act (LASPO). The Act attempted to reduce legal aid services for non-residents. The High Court blocked legislation regarding non-residents for reasons explained by Lord Justice Moses: 'Within the system provided by Laspo, the United Kingdom is not permitted to discriminate against non-residents on the grounds that to do so might save costs'. Moses goes on:

> Using powers that were never his to exercise, the Lord Chancellor (Chris Grayling) has attempted to refashion the legal-aid scheme into an instrument of discrimination so that many of the cases (Parliament) itself identified as most worthy of support could never be taken...(I)t is simply unacceptable in a country where all are equal in the eyes of the law. Legal aid is, and must remain, the means to safeguard equality in our courts, regardless of people's origins, nationality or place of residence.[92]

The government's cutbacks in legal aid services to residents continued, demonstrating that not everyone has recognition before the law.

In 2014, the High Court ruled that Lord Chancellor Chris Grayling (Tory) acted unlawfully over his non-disclosure of two reports published during the consultation process. Justice Burnett decreed the measures were 'so unfair' as to be unlawful. In the same year, the Law Society and other groups appealed against the government's decision to cut legal aid to the bare bones. But a year later, the Court of Appeal dismissed the case. Law Society president Andrew Caplen calls their decision 'a devastating blow. We remain concerned that vulnerable people may not be able to obtain legal representation if they are accused of wrongdoing'. In 2015, the High Court upheld the government's decision to slash police station and court magistrate contracts in England and Wales from 1,600 to 527.[93]

In 2016, Justice Secretary Michael Gove (Tory) tried to again cut back on legal aid for non-residents. The Public Law Project took the government to the High Court, which ruled against the government. High Court President Lord Neuberger ruled that the government's move was beyond their legal powers (*ultra vires*), 'and unjustifiably discriminatory and so in breach of common law and the Human Rights Act 1998'. A year later, the Howard League for Penal Reform, the Prisoners' Advice Service and the Equality and Human Rights Commission brought a case against the government. This time, three judges ruled unanimously against further cuts to legal aid for prisoners.[94]

In its report (2016) to the UN High Commissioner for Human Rights, the Equality and Human Rights Commission writes:

Restrictions in the scope of legal aid in England and Wales will have a significant impact on the ability of people to access justice when their rights under ICESCR (International Covenant on Economic, Social and Cultural Rights) have been breached. The way in which legal aid is administered also impedes access to justice. The UK Government should monitor the actual impact of these changes, including on potentially vulnerable groups...(The investigating team) noted a particular concern about evidential requirements for accessing legal aid in private family law cases, which has led to a large proportion of women not being able to access civil legal aid to bring cases in relation to domestic violence.[95]

Chapter 7

Equal...if you're white and middle class

Article 7

All are equal before the law and are entitled without any discrimination to equal protection of the law. All are entitled to equal protection against any discrimination in violation of this Declaration and against any incitement to such discrimination.

The Howard League for Penal Reform writes (2009): 'Prison is demonstrably a highly selective tool for social control. It disproportionately targets black and ethnic minorities, the poor, the young, the troubled and the troubling. Prison...is rarely deployed as a punishment for those responsible for state and corporate crimes'. The report notes that '(t)hose we punish are largely the poor and disadvantaged, those with mental health needs and drug or alcohol addictions. We demonstrate little concern over our widespread use of prison and punishment for children'.[96]

Persons from disadvantaged backgrounds are far more likely than their privileged counterparts to end up in prison or face fines and community service. The Blair government's Social Exclusion Unit reported that by 2002, 27% of prisoners had been placed in care as children compared to 2% of the non-prison population. Almost half had been child runaways. More than 50% of male prisoners had no qualifications. Forty-nine per cent were expelled from school and 80% of prisoners had reading/writing skills at or below the level of the average 11-year-old. Class prejudice is symptomatic of the wider problem concerning lack of rights for the underprivileged. Drawing on the report, the peer-reviewed *Internet Journal of Criminology* notes: 'Over two thirds of prisoners were unemployed prior to being sentenced, compared with just 5% of the general population; furthermore 75% of prisoners have no employment to go to upon release. Of those in prison during 2002, 80% possessed mental health problems...(A)lmost half had a long standing illness or disability and over 60% were regular drug users prior to being sentenced'. The journal notes 'the incarceration of a socially excluded superfluous population'.[97]

Ten years later, Britain's prison population had reached a record 88,179. Sir Suma Chakrabarti, the Justice Ministry's Permanent Secretary, said that the Tory-Liberal government's 'U-turn on sentencing reforms means the number of criminals in prison is likely to remain near record levels'. The Equality and Human Rights Commission (EHRC) 'found that five times more black people than white people per head of population in England and Wales are imprisoned', not much change since the more overtly racist 1960s. The racial disparity is less to do with crime and more to do with police and judicial victimization. The EHRC (2010) also states: 'On the streets, black people were subjected to...an "excess" of 145,000 stop and searches in 2008', even though blacks constitute 2.2% of the population. Despite this, they 'made up 15% of people stopped by police'.[98]

The charity Inquest notes excessive deaths of blacks-ethnic minorities (BEMs) compared to whites in police custody. Between the years 1990 to early-2017, there were 161 BEM deaths in police custody and as a result of police shootings. Turning to convictions, the Institute for Race Relations (IRR) notes that a 2011 meta-analysis of 1 million court records shows black offenders 44% more likely than whites 'to be given a prison sentence for driving offences, 38 per cent more likely for public order offences or possession of a weapon and 27 per cent more likely for possession of drugs'. The IRR concludes that British Asians are 19% 'more likely than white people to be given a prison sentence for shoplifting and 41 per cent more likely for drugs offences'.[99]

The *Guardian* also reports that 14% of the prison population is Muslim, most of them ethnic Asians, despite the fact that Asians constitute just 4.8% of the population in England and Wales. This compounds an earlier Human Rights Watch report from the post-9/11 Blair era. It condemns the Metropolitan Police for victimizing Asians (mainly ethnic Pakistanis and Bangladeshis) under the Terrorism Act 2000. 'Of the 185,086 people stopped and searched by the (Met) under section 44', which unlawfully[a] permits public stops and searches, in 2008-09, 'around 58 per cent defined themselves as white (107,853); around 11 per cent (21,496) as black; around 16 per cent (29,716) as Asian; around 4 per cent (8,548) grouped as "Chinese" or "other"'.[100]

THE 'ABLED' BOYS' CLUB

Notice that Article 7 of the UDHR prohibits discrimination in general, not just in the legal system. What about gender discrimination in the UK?

In 2008, the UN Convention on the Elimination of All Forms of Discrimination Against Women found that 'British women are under-represented in Parliament, paid less than men at work and (are) increasingly being sent to prison for committing minor offences'. It concluded that women's pay was on average 17% lower than men's.[101]

As noted, 6 years later the UN Human Rights Council's Special Rapporteur, Rashida Manjoo, visited the UK and concluded: 'there is a boys' club, sexist culture that exists' in Britain. To expand on what Manjoo said: 'Access to trauma services, financial support and housing are crucial, yet current reforms to the funding and benefits system continue to adversely impact women's ability to address safety and other relevant issues'. Other issues highlighted include sexual bullying in schools, sexualized media and concerns over the Yarl's Wood 'holding facility' for women and families facing deportation. The latter would have been a concern, but, as noted, the Home Office refused to agree to grant Manjoo access.[102]

What about people with disabilities? The Tory-led austerity measures (2010-present) discriminate against the poor and needy to such an extent that, under pressure from UK disability rights groups, the UN launched an inquiry. In 2007, the UK signed the Optional Protocol on the Convention on the Rights of Persons with Disabilities. As noted, the UK became the first country to be investigated by the UN Committee on the Rights of Persons with Disabilities for alleged violations of the protocol. The Committee launched an official inquiry in 2015. A year later, it concluded that the Cameron-led government committed 'grave or systematic violations of the rights of persons with disabilities'. It goes on to say that

> several measures have disproportionally and adversely affected the rights of persons with disabilities...Measures resulting in reduction of support provided to meet the extra cost of disability, denial of reasonable accommodation in assessment procedures and realization of the right to employment have had a discriminatory effect on persons with disabilities.[103]

Nearly half a million disability benefits claimants were forcibly put onto a new social security scheme, which included attempts to force them into work (Employment and Support Allowance), leading to nearly 42,000 economic sanctions being imposed. The charity Crisis reports that sanctions have increased homelessness.[104]

Chapter 8

Justice for some

Article 8

Everyone has the right to an effective remedy by the competent national tribunals for acts violating the fundamental rights granted him by the constitution or by law.

There is no database of persons who a) would like justice but haven't the means, knowhow or confidence to seek it or b) have sought justice and failed due to institutional constraints. Observation alone proves that the majority of people who feel discriminated against have no recourse to justice. Under 30% of crime in the UK is solved, school and workplace bullying is endemic and the government has shielded itself from reprisals from those whom it targets by cutting back on legal aid.

There all sorts of measures for gauging injustice in the UK. Take the issue of violence against women. According to Article 8, everyone should have the right to take their abusers to court, should they wish. But spending cuts and a culture that favours the male defendant often prevents women from getting justice.

According to the British government, more than one quarter of women and over 10% of men in England and Wales have experienced domestic abuse, including physical, sexual and/or psychological. This translates to 4.5 million women and 2.2 million men between the ages of 16 and 59. The National Society for the Protection of Children reckons that one quarter of under-18s also experience domestic abuse. In a single year, 1.3 million women and 600,000 men are victims of domestic abuse. There are a number of legal safeguards against domestic abuse, including criminal (for example, The Serious Crime Act 2015) and civil (for example, non-molestation orders). The government's Home

Office (2016) published a four-year strategy to end violence against girls and women. The government also created a Violence Against Women and Girls Service Transformation Fund (2017).[105]

Due to Tory-imposed austerity, 17% of women's refuges closed in the UK between 2010 and 2016. Women's Aid, which the government consulted as part of plans to increase funding for vulnerable women, says that 155 women per day were being refused by refuges due to lack of funding. In 2017, Sunderland became the first major UK city not have a single woman's refuge centre. The Wearside Women in Need group ran for 35 years and was due to close in June 2017 when the council planned to terminate the contract due to lack of funds. According to the organization, 1,600 women a year, many of them from ethnic and religious minorities, rely on the service.[106]

With regard to the police record, there is no police-judicial definition of 'domestic violence' and records are not centrally collected, says the government. The cases of domestic violence recorded by police in England and Wales have grown from 650,000 in the year 2008 to over 1 million in 2015. According to Women's Aid, every week two women in England and Wales are killed by their partners. Women's Aid also notes that it is impossible to tell how many women are being abused domestically due to fear on the part of victims and police failure to log reports. Rights of Women, a group dedicating itself to helping women with legal issues, reports that 40% of affected women are unable to provide the requisite evidence of their abuse, such as supporting evidence from doctors, signs of physical abuse and video evidence. This limits the number of cases in which women get justice.[107]

Rights of Women says that changes to legal aid (April 2013) put a 24-month limit on claims. The Divisional Court dismissed the case brought by Rights of Women, that these changes would prevent the most vulnerable from attaining legal help and ultimately protection and justice. Director Emma Scott says: 'women...continue to be denied access to justice by the legal aid regulations. (W)e are devastated by the outcome of our legal challenge'. Andrew Caplen of the Law Society says: 'Without legal aid women are being forced to face their perpetrators in court without legal representation'. Pressure from Rights of Women led to a Court of Appeals decision in February 2016 to overturn the ruling.[108]

Chapter 9

Land of the free?

Article 9

No one shall be subjected to arbitrary arrest, detention or exile.

Earlier, we saw how the police and courts discriminate against ethnic minorities, including arbitrary arrests and detentions. Following the New Labour government's effort to extend detention in custody without charge to 42 days, following the 9/11 attacks, the House of Lords overruled the government. Currently, police can only hold an individual for 24 hours, apply to hold for 36 or, in the case of suspected murder, hold for up to 96 hours. Under the Criminal Justice Act 2003, a person can be held for up to 14 days. Under the Terrorism Act 2006, a person can be held for 28 days.[109]

New Labour's Anti-Terrorism Crime and Security Act 2001 enables the police to indefinitely detain foreign nationals on suspicion of being a risk to national security. The rights group Justice says that between December 2001 and April 2005, 17 individuals were detained under the Act. But Britons have also been subject to arbitrary detention.[110]

BABAR AHMAD

Babar Ahmad is a British citizen. He was born in Pakistan and grew up in Tooting, London. His father worked as a Foreign Office clerk. Ahmad served in the Royal Air Force cadets and at the age of 21 fought Serbs in Bosnia as part of the *jihad*. At that time, the US and Britain were organizing groups of terrorists to fight a proxy war in Bosnia. There is no suggestion that Ahmad is a terrorist or was involved in the British-US proxy war. In 2003, Ahmad was arrested by the Metropolitan Police's counterterrorism unit and extradited to the US, where he was convicted of materially supporting the Taliban. The extradition was a political show-trial. Mayor Boris Johnson, not the most sympathetic of men, acknowledged that Ahmad should have been tried in the UK. But there was no evidence linking him to terrorism, hence the extradition.[111]

The British police tortured Ahmad, admitting liability and paying him damages. They groped his genitals, squeezed his handcuffs so tight that he screamed and punched him in the face repeatedly, causing 73 injuries. The cuffs left scars. Custody Sgt Thomas Martin described Ahmad's handcuffs injuries as the worst he'd seen in 30 years. Ahmad was held for *8 years without trial* by the British police before being extradited to the US. He was stripped, blindfolded, shackled and sentenced to 12 years solitary confinement in a maximum-security prison. After serving 3 years, having pleaded guilty to conspiracy and providing material support for terrorism, Ahmad was freed and allowed to return to the UK. Showing its contempt for British common law and the Universal Declaration, the British Home Office said that after allegedly committing these crimes, 'he finally faced justice and was put behind bars (in the US)'.[112]

JULIAN ASSANGE

A UN body opined that Briton's best-known political prisoner has been arbitrarily detained since 2010, when he was put under house arrest.

Julian Hawkins (Assange) was born in Australia in 1971. His mother later married one Richard Assange. Julian Assange, as he was later known, began hacking under the name Mendax in his teens. Assange and his colleagues hacked into numerous companies and US agencies, including the Pentagon, NASA and the US Navy. By 1993, the Victoria Police Child Exploitation Unit was receiving technical assistance from Assange. In 1996, Assange pleaded guilty to 25 charges brought by the US, including hacking. He was fined. A decade later, he and his colleagues founded WikiLeaks.

In August 2010, two Swedish women accused Assange of sexual assault. The case was closed due to lack of evidence and Assange left Sweden for London. He was then wanted for questioning by the Swedish special prosecutor, who tried to reopen the case, on two counts: one of coercion and the other of so-called lesser-degree rape. Assange agreed to be questioned via video link from the UK, where he was based; but the Swedish authorities refused and sought his extradition. Assange considered this to be a political manoeuvre to extradite him to the US from Sweden over his WikiLeaks publications. The rape allegations, he believed, were a ruse. The statute of limitations concerning so-called lesser-degree rape will expire in 2020. In December 2010, the Swedish prosecutor issued an international arrest warrant for Assange, who was detained for 10 days in isolation in Wandsworth Prison, UK. Assange was then put under house arrest for 550 days.

In 2012, Assange successfully sought political asylum in the Ecuadorian Embassy in London, where he has been effectively imprisoned ever since. In December 2015, the UN Working Group on Arbitrary Detention launched an investigation. In early-2016, three out of the five members of the Working Group concluded: 'Assange was arbitrarily detained by the Governments of Sweden and the United Kingdom...(T)he Working Group recognized that Mr. Assange is entitled to his freedom of movement and to compensation'. But the UN law is non-binding in the UK. The Working Group further concluded that 'Assange has not been able to leave the Ecuadorian Embassy and is subject to extensive surveillance by the British police'.[113]

Then-Foreign Secretary Philip Hammond called the Working Group's conclusion 'frankly...a ridiculous finding'. The British government added: 'This changes nothing. We completely reject any claim that Julian Assange is a victim of arbitrary detention.

The UK has already made clear to the UN that we will formally contest the working group's opinion'.[114]

Chapter 10

Secret courts

Article 10

Everyone is entitled in full equality to a fair and public hearing by an independent and impartial tribunal, in the determination of his rights and obligations and of any criminal charge against him.

In Britain, asylum seekers, foreigners seeking compensation from the government and individuals allegedly suspected of posing a national security risk can have secret evidence brought against them in secret courts.

According to a report by the rights group Justice, criteria for evidence has been historically more 'flexible' in civil cases than in criminal cases. When the Tories adopted the Civil Evidence Act 1995, hearsay became admissible. Since New Labour came to power in 1997, the government adopted 14 pieces of legislation out to the year 2011, allowing secret evidence (that is, evidence that the accused cannot see) to be used in court. The report traces the growth of secret evidence back to the Special Immigration Appeals Commission, established in 1997 in response to a European Court of Human Rights judgment (*Chahal v United Kingdom*). (Chahal sought asylum in the UK because he claimed that he would face persecution in his native India. The government sought to deny him asylum on the grounds of national security.)[115]

The commission was the first statutory provision allowing secret evidence to be used in a court in Britain. The commission became 'the model for its use in all subsequent civil proceedings', says Justice. The Special Immigration Appeals Commission introduced closed material procedures (CMPs). Under Part 4 of the Anti-Terrorism Crime and Security Act 2001, CMPs are frequently used. For instance: One Abu Rideh was accused of supporting the Taliban by the British deep state, including by a member of the so-called security services, Witness B. Rideh's counsel asked, '(I)s he (Rideh) entitled to know what is alleged against him(?)', referring to certain documents. Witness B replied: 'All the evidence there is closed'.[116]

In 2013, the Tory-led coalition government introduced the Justice and Security Act, which expanded CMPs to the area of rendition, torture, data and intelligence. (Rendition means the kidnap and torture of alleged terrorism suspects. The US is by far the main perpetrator of rendition, but the UK assists America by providing bases and refuelling sites.) In the same year, two men, Erol Incedal and Rarmoul Bouhadjar, were charged with conspiracy to commit terrorism. They were later convicted but retried. A fresh jury cleared Incedal. The Crown Prosecution Service attempted to keep their names out of the media because, in their words, '(should) factors of concern be ventilated in a public trial...(the prosecution would be) presented with representations (to drop the charges on the grounds of national security). (The BBC reporter's additions are in brackets. After the police confiscated reporters' notepads following a media gag, the Court of Appeal upheld the government's decision to keep it a secret trial.[117]

In 2014, the European Parliament's Committee on Civil Liberties, Justice and Home Affairs (LIBE) published a lengthy report, singling out the UK for criticism over the use of secret evidence against individuals. Although the report also criticizes Germany, Holland, Spain and Sweden, LIBE says: 'The United Kingdom stands as an exception in the European landscape when examining the use of secrecy during trials. The use of 'closed material procedures' (CMPs) in judicial proceedings is provided for in national legislation. CMPs allow sensitive intelligence material to be introduced in secret hearings in which only the judge and special advocates have access to the material'.[118]

In 2017, two Pakistanis alleged they were tortured with the knowledge of the British establishment. Amanatullah Ali and Yunus Rahmatullah were held by the illegal British occupiers of Iraq in 2004 before being sent by the US to Bagram AFB in Afghanistan, where they spent 10 years as prisoners. The UK Ministry of Defence and Foreign Office have been allowed by Justice Leggatt to present secret evidence to the court, which the two men will not get to examine. Omran Belhadi is a lawyer working at Reprieve who assisted the plaintiffs. He said of the decision: 'This is a dark day for British justice. The government is insisting on secret hearings – concealed even from the victims – to continue covering up its error' in supporting America's rendition programme.[119]

One might say crime instead of error.

Chapter 11

First degree murder

Article 11

(1) Everyone charged with a penal offence has the right to be presumed innocent until proved guilty according to law in a public trial at which he has had all the guarantees necessary for his defence.

(2) No one shall be held guilty of any penal offence on account of any act or omission which did not constitute a penal offence, under national or international law, at the time when it was committed. Nor shall a heavier penalty be imposed than the one that was applicable at the time the penal offence was committed.

The age-old common law presumption of innocence has faced a slight setback in the so-called 'war on terror'. Since US drone operators killed Afghan civilians in 2002, followed by Yemini civilians in the same year, America has murdered about 2,500 people: 98% of whom were civilians, according to US military analyses. Even those who are not civilian are entitled under international and domestic US-British law to be tried for alleged involvement in terrorism. The sheer volume of Islamophobia in Western media, coupled with the incremental passive acceptance of civilian-targeting drone warfare, has led to a situation in which the US and British governments murder people with impunity. As this book concerns domestic violations of the Universal Declaration, I shall mostly focus on British citizens murdered by British drone operators.[120]

The UN Special Rapporteur on Extrajudicial, Summary or Arbitrary Execution, Philip Alston, writes: 'A State killing is legal only if it is required to protect life (making lethal force *proportionate*) and there is no other means, such as capture or nonlethal incapacitation, of preventing that threat to life (making lethal force *necessary*)'. So, a person in Afghanistan, for example, cannot be killed lawfully by a British drone operator on the pretence that the person is about to pose an imminent threat to the UK, unless for instance the person is about to give an order over the phone to, for instance, a terror cell in Briton instructing it to detonate a bomb.[121]

MURDERING ITS OWN

The British state murdering 'its own people' is nothing new. In the 1970s, the Ministry of Defence waged a dirty war in Northern Ireland. Units from the Military Reaction Force murdered Protestants and Catholics as a part of strategy of tension. Northern Irish persons murdered and/or shot by the MRF include: Patrick McVeigh (shot in the back), John and Gerry Conway (travelling to a fruit stall), Aiden McAloon and Eugene Devlin (travelling in a taxi), Joe Smith, Hugh Kenny, Patrick Murray and Tommy Shaw (killed in drive-by shootings) and Daniel Rooney and Brendan Brennan (walking on a road).[122]

The British government does in fact possess the proverbial licence to kill. It is a 'licence' granted to itself and one not grounded in international law. Targeted killings (murder) hitherto depended on the authorization of the Secretary of State. The Intelligence Services Act 1994, Section 7(1), frees intelligence operatives from liability in acts of killing abroad, 'if the act is one which is authorised to be done by virtue of an authorisation given by the Secretary of State'. In the case of Reyaad Khan, the killings were not carried out by MI6 (which is covered by the Intelligence Services Act 1994), but by the Royal Air Force.[123]

In 2015, the government started murdering Britons allegedly suspected of involvement in terrorism, making no attempt to apprehend them and put them on trial, as international law requires.

In August 2015, Reyaad Khan and Abdul Raqib Amin were travelling in a vehicle in Raqqa, Syria. RAF drone operators ended their lives. Then-PM David Cameron told Parliament that Khan was the target (murdered) and Amin was killed alongside him (manslaughter). A third unidentified, alleged Islamic State fighter was killed with them, though the third person was not 'identified as a UK national'. By implication, the third person's life is not important, hence no details emerged.[124]

Cameron claimed the killings were 'an act of self-defence', because Khan was 'involved in actively recruiting ISIL sympathisers and seeking to orchestrate specific and barbaric attacks against the West, including directing a number of planned terrorist attacks right here in Britain, such as plots to attack high-profile public commemorations'. But Cameron also revealed that Khan was *not* a threat to the UK: 'there was nothing to suggest that Reyaad Khan would ever leave Syria'. If Cameron is to be believed, Khan was issuing instructions to terror cells in the UK. But if this is the case, it therefore becomes a matter for the British police.[125]

The pretext for the murder was later changed by the UK's Permanent Representative to the UN, Matthew Rycroft, who wrote that the killings were somehow justified in the 'collective self-defence' of Iraq, where Briton is supposedly helping the government to defeat ISIS. The trouble is that Khan was not in Iraq when he was killed. Inverting international legal norms, Secretary of State for Defence, Michael Fallon, 'who authorised the lethal drone strike' (*Press and Journal*), appealed to Article 51 of the UN Charter, the right of collective and/or individual self-defence. Attorney General Jeremy Wright's advice has not been published, indicating that the killings are violations of domestic and international law.[126]

It later transpired that the RAF is working its way through a 'kill list' of alleged British terror suspects fighting with ISIS in Iraq and Syria. Both jets and drones are used; the latter are controlled by operators in RAF Waddington, Lincolnshire. 'When we know where they are we kill them', said an MoD spokesperson. The 'kill list' revelations prompted Lord Macdonald, former Director of Public Prosecutions, to co-sign a letter to PM May, calling for the release of the government's Intelligence and Security Committee report into the murder of Reyaad Khan and names of other targeted suspects.[127]

Lucy Powell MP and Kirsten Oswald MP, both co-chairs of the informal All-Party Parliamentary Group, called for a debate on Britain's use of targeted murder. Defence Secretary Fallon who authorized the murder of Khan claimed that by February 2017, 85 Britons had been killed in Syria, but it wasn't clear if this meant as part of the RAF's kill list.[128]

Chapter 12

We're watching you

Article 12

No one shall be subjected to arbitrary interference with his privacy, family, home or correspondence, nor to attacks upon his honour and reputation. Everyone has the right to the protection of the law against such interference or attacks.

British subjects have always been spied on. The original ordinance establishing the Post Office stated that it would be the ultimate safeguard against those with ill-designs on the Empire, implying that mail would be systematically inspected. When the first telephone lines were established, they were rapidly wired to intelligence listening posts, as journalist Duncan Campbell has discovered. (Campbell's office was raided by police under the Official Secrets Act when he obtained info on the Zircon spy satellite.)[129]

After WWII, Britain became part of the USA's Five Eyes (with Australia, New Zealand and Canada). The United Kingdom's Government Communications Headquarters' official mandate is to collect information to protect Britain's economic security, hence the mass spying on businesspeople. Canadian agent Mike Frost revealed that the Five Eyes can even pick up conversations through baby monitors. The US and Britain has a system known as Echelon, in which key words spoken or typed (for example, the name of a politician) automatically draw attention from intelligence staff who then record or listen in on phone calls. Microsoft was allegedly developed with US National Security Agency (NSA) technology to send keystrokes to the US intelligence agencies.[130]

In 1997, the US Space Command announced its intention

to rule the world by force: 'Full Spectrum Dominance'. A core component of Full Spectrum Dominance is 'info dominance'. These matters, long familiar to researchers and activists, were finally brought to mass public attention by NSA whistle-blower Edward Snowden who confirmed that everything everyone says or does on a communications system – phone, internet, email, text, smart phone and so on – is recorded by the US and British intelligence agencies in mass data grabs. One operation (Optic Nerve) involved the UK MoD spying on users by hacking into and using their webcams. It was later revealed that the MoD was hacking into people's smart televisions and recording conversations.[131]

Despite all the nonsense about anti-encryption and back-door technologies that the British government wants Apple to use in its smart phones to enable access to communications, *Der Spiegel* revealed years ago, citing top NSA officials, that the NSA can and does hack into smart phones, record conversations, take pictures and (even when the device is switched off) track users' locations. The internet and smart technologies have made mass spying not only easy, but big business.[132]

In 2014, the government adopted the Data Retention and Investigatory Powers Act (DRIP). The UN High Commissioner for Human Rights, Navi Pillay, condemned the Act as 'de facto coercion of private sector companies to provide sweeping access to information and data relating to private individuals without the latter's knowledge or consent'. But the report for the Human Rights Council went further and generally condemned the UK's mass data collection as contrary to international law. The report specifically references Article 12, above: 'As recalled by the General Assembly in its resolution 68/167, international human rights law provides the universal framework against which any interference in individual privacy rights must be assessed'.[133]

Pillay also criticized the Cameron government's efforts to ram DRIP through Parliament: 'it's difficult to see how the

UK can now justify rushing through wide-reaching emergency legislation which may not fully address the concerns raised by the court, at time when there are proceedings ongoing by the UK's own investigative powers tribunal on these very issues'. At the time of the bill's ascension, the courts of the following countries had struck down similar bills, leaving the UK in its usual splendid isolation: Austria, Bulgaria, Cyprus, the Czech Republic, Germany, Romania and Slovenia.[134]

In 2015, Joseph Cannataci, the UN Special Rapporteur on Privacy said of the UK: 'Your oversight mechanism's a joke, and a rather bad joke at its citizens' expense'. In January 2016, UN human rights experts 'called for a comprehensive review of the (UK's) draft Investigatory Powers bill, warning that if adopted...could threaten the rights to freedom of expression and association'. In March 2016, Cannataci submitted a report to the Human Rights Council on surveillance in the digital age. The report contained a section on the UK's Investigatory Powers Bill and recommended:[135]

disproportionate, privacy-intrusive measures such as bulk surveillance and bulk hacking as contemplated in the Investigatory Powers Bill be outlawed rather than legitimised. It would appear that the serious and possibly unintended consequences of legitimising bulk interception and bulk hacking are not being fully appreciated by the UK Government.[136]

Chapter 13

Freedom of movement

Article 13

(1) Everyone has the right to freedom of movement and residence within the borders of each state.

(2) Everyone has the right to leave any country, including his own, and to return to his country.

What happens if the government chooses to suspect you of some link to some crime, provides no evidence to you or to the court and restricts your freedom of movement with electronic tagging?

In 2005, the New Labour government introduced the Prevention of Terrorism Act. The Act implemented a form of indefinite house arrest and electronic tagging based on alleged suspicion of terrorism or connections to terrorism. Authorities seeking to issue control orders against an individual needed only the permission of the Home Secretary, based on hearsay: not the permission of evidence-based courts. These were known as control orders. In its report reviewing Britain's alleged counterterrorism legislation, Amnesty International (2010):

> considers that the control orders regime, with the procedures and range of potential measures as currently legislated and applied in the UK, is not compatible with the UK's human rights obligations under international law. The judicial procedures by which the imposition of a control order can be challenged are inconsistent with fundamental fair trial rights. The court can consider secret material to support the claim that the individual is or has been involved in terrorism-related activity, and that the measures imposed are necessary to protect members of the public.[137]

Control orders prevent the alleged suspect from knowing why they are being held.

A House of Commons Library report confirms that British nationals and non-nationals alike can be subjected to control orders. Between 2005 and 2009, the government claims to have put 45 individuals on control orders. Liberty and security safeguards are included in the European Convention on Human Rights (ECHR, Article 5), to which Britain is party in 2017. In 2007, the House of Lords ruled that certain aspects of the control orders regime (which consists of derogating and non-derogating[b] control orders) breach human rights, including Article 5 of the ECHR. Despite this, the courts upheld the use of control orders. Under Article 6 of the ECHR, the Lords challenged the issue of closed materials in 2009. The court decided that targets have the right to see alleged evidence against them, but *de facto* evidence often remained withheld.[138]

To give one case: Cerie Bullivant was a student nurse. He spent 2 years under house arrest after being detained in 2006 when he attempted to board a flight for Syria, where he claims that he wanted to learn Arabic and volunteer in an orphanage. The government alleged he was en route to Iraq to fight against the illegal Anglo-American occupiers; but the alleged evidence was never presented to Bullivant. Despite being cleared of any suspected wrongdoing, Bullivant 'was required to wear an electronic tag, observe a curfew, report daily to police and to expect his home to be raided at any time. The regime forced him to drop out of college, made it impossible for him to find a job, caused the collapse of his marriage and led to him being shunned by friends and family', says the *Independent*, which covered the story. 'He said he still faces abuse and suspicion to this day'. Bullivant himself says: 'You can't win a war on terror by terrorising a community. Control orders are so counterproductive within the Muslim community. It's like internment with the Irish. You are throwing fuel on the flames of anyone who is going to be radicalised'.[139]

In 2011, the Tory-Liberal government introduced the Terrorism Prevention and Investigation Measures (TPIMs) Act. TPIMs were supposed to replace control orders. The Lords-Commons Joint Committee on Human Rights notes that TPIMs were designed to place under house arrest individuals who can neither be tried nor deported. How is it possible that an individual can be neither tried nor deported, unless the government is colluding with them and seeking to hide this fact from the public?[c] The Lords-Commons report says: 'Our post-legislative scrutiny has failed to find any evidence that TPIMs have led in practice to any more criminal prosecutions of terrorism suspects'. The Lords-Commons report goes on to note that TPIMs are no better in this respect than control orders. 'This confirms the concerns we expressed in our scrutiny Reports on the Bill that the replacement for control orders were not "investigative" in any meaningful sense'.[140]

On TPIMs, Amnesty, which so criticized control orders, also says that TPIMs are little different from control orders. The TPIMs:

> allow the Home Secretary to order that people are subject to significant curtailments to their liberty, freedom of movement, association and privacy - all without charge or trial. On the basis of secret evidence individuals could be tagged and forced to remain within their home under overnight curfews; have restrictions placed on the use of mobile phones, the internet or talking to named people; and prevented from working in certain jobs or travelling overseas.

Amnesty's Tim Hancock describes TPIMs as a 'cheap make-over' for control orders. In essence, they allow for more individuals to endure what Bullivant experienced.[141]

Chapter 14

Send 'em back!

Article 14

(1) Everyone has the right to seek and to enjoy in other countries asylum from persecution.

(2) This right may not be invoked in the case of prosecutions genuinely arising from non-political crimes or from acts contrary to the purposes and principles of the United Nations.

Britain's got talent at creating refugees. As a matter of historical record: By promising a homeland to both Arabs and Jews and then betraying both, Britain helped create 5 million Palestinian refugees. By invading Iraq illegally, the UK created 4.4 million. By training, arming and organizing terrorists in Syria and Libya, and by bombing both countries, the UK created a further 11 million. By training the armed forces of Colombia, Britain is contributing to Colombia's internal 4 million refugee crisis. By training and arming terrorists in Afghanistan in 1979 'to draw the Russians into the Afghan trap' (Jimmy Carter's National Security Advisor), Britain helped create 3 million refugees in neighbouring Pakistan and Iran.

Britain doesn't like it when a comparatively tiny number of these refugees attempt to enter the UK: this despite the fact that Britain has a legal obligation to accept asylum seekers under the Refugee Convention 1951. In July 2001, the UN High Commissioner for Refugees, Ruud Lubbers, criticized Australia, Austria, Denmark, Italy and the UK for political attitudes towards refugees and asylum seekers, especially during election cycles. 'Statistics are frequently manipulated, facts are taken out of context, and the character of asylum-seekers as a group is often distorted in order to present them as a terrible threat'. Lubbers goes on to note that '(a)sylum-seekers make a perfect target for people who want to invoke the age-old prejudice against foreigners. Asylum-seekers can't answer back. 'Illegal'; 'bogus'; 'flood'; 'fraudulent'; 'criminal'; 'scrounger' and 'trafficking' are all are words commonly paired with the term 'asylum-seeker''.[142]

In 2013, the Tory government led by PM Cameron drafted an immigration bill. The UN High Commissioner for Refugees, António Guterres, sent a briefing note to MPs in which he said: 'The provisions of the bill appear likely to result in asylum-seekers, refugees and beneficiaries of subsidiary protection being stigmatised in the public mind and in their being denied access to housing or bank accounts'. Guterres goes on to say that:

> (t)he UN high commissioner for refugees is concerned that if introduced, such measures could contribute towards a climate of misunderstanding and ethnic profiling that could undermine the longer-term prospects for integration of such persons and prove detrimental to social cohesion.[143]

When 'Europe', not the hundreds of thousands of desperate men, women and children fleeing death, destruction and poverty, but Europe, faced a refugee 'crisis' between 2015-17, far-right pundit Katie Hopkins referred to refugees as cockroaches. She also said that they should be shot.

In response to Hopkins's column, Zeid Ra'ad Al Hussein, the UN High Commissioner for Human Rights, said that the British media have a track-record of 'decades of sustained and unrestrained anti-foreigner abuse, misinformation and distortion'. Zeid also noted that '(t)he Nazi media described people their masters wanted to eliminate as rats and cockroaches'. Zeid goes on to say that '(t)his type of language is clearly inflammatory and unacceptable, especially in a national newspaper. *The Sun*'s editors took an editorial decision to publish this article, and – if it is found in breach of the law – should be held responsible along with the author'. It was only when Hopkins denigrated Jewish people with talk of a 'Final Solution' to deal with Muslims (a claim she denies) that LBC radio fired her.[144]

But the much bigger picture is that Britain has been denying refugees asylum for decades.

Despite mass-media propaganda concerning an unprecedented refugee crisis between 2015-17, the House of Commons Library confirms: 'The number of asylum applications to the UK peaked in 2002 at 84,132. After that the number fell sharply to reach a twenty year low point of 17,916 in 2010, before rising again to reach 32,733 in 2015. The number fell in 2016, to 30,603'. In the years following a series of illegal wars led by Tony Blair's New Labour government, Serbia (1999), Afghanistan (2001) and Iraq (2003), Britain increased its number of asylum application refusals. The House of Commons report goes on to note that '(t)he percentage of asylum applicants refused at initial decision reached its highest point at 88% in 2004. After that, the percentage of applicants refused at initial decision fell to 59% in 2014, before increasing to 66% in 2016'.[145]

Continuing with the shocking record under New Labour, the Refugee Council states: 'Since 2005 most people recognised as refugees are only given permission to stay in the UK for 5 years and can have their case reviewed at any time'. It notes that this situation 'makes it difficult for them to make decisions about their future, to find work and make definite plans for their life in the UK'. The Refugee Council goes on: 'The UK asylum system is strictly controlled and complex. It is very difficult to get asylum. The process is extremely tough and the majority of people's claims are turned down'. It goes on to say that, '(o)n average about 65% of women's asylum claims are rejected each year'. The Refugee Council also notes that '(a) high number of initial decisions made by the Home Office on asylum cases are wrong.

In 2013, the courts overturned 25% of negative decisions after they were appealed'.[146]

But as the House of Commons Library notes, the number of asylum seekers who appeal is no more than a third, so the total number of successful appeals is 8.3%.

LOCK 'EM UP!

In addition to violating Article 14 above, Britain also violates the provision against arbitrary detention, discussed in Chapter 9.

Concerning refugees, immigrants and asylum seekers, Britain has 12 immigration removal centres, holding a total of 3,500 migrants and asylum seekers for indefinite periods, including immigrants who have lived in the UK for decades and find themselves told to leave by the Home Office. The centres are prisons. Depending on the centre in question, detainees' labour is exploited (for example, cooking, cleaning), facilities are dirty, suicide watch is substandard, medical complaints are often ignored or ridiculed, bullying is rife and long spells in isolation are common.[147]

Oxford University's Migration Observatory cites the UK as one of Europe's main detainers of immigrants and asylum seekers. It notes that '(o)ver 1,000 children were detained for the purpose of immigration control in 2009, and this number was reduced to just under 130 in 2011. It rose to 242 in 2012, before falling to 71 in 2016'. In a report entitled *State-sponsored cruelty* (2016), Medical Justice notes that despite pledges by the Tory-Liberal coalition government, the detention of immigrant-refugee children in Britain's inhuman holding centres continued well into the Tory government's term (starting 2015). The report investigated 141 children held in the UK. Among other horrors, including witnessing and experiencing physical abuse, it finds that of the children investigated:[148]

(Seventy-four) were reported to have been psychologically

harmed as a result of being detained. Symptoms included bed wetting and loss of bowel control, heightened anxiety, food refusal, withdrawal and disinterest, and persistent crying. 34 children exhibited signs of developmental regression, and six children expressed suicidal ideation either whilst or after they were detained. Three girls attempted to end their own lives. The effects of detention continued, in many cases, after children were released and some teachers drew attention to worsening school performance. One child was reported to be holding a silent vigil, looking out of his window in the mornings, at the time he had been subjected to a dawn raid (by the British immigration authorities). [149]

Phil Miller is the author of exposés of British abuse of asylum seekers in detention. Writing about the Verne immigration removal centre on the Isle of Portland, Dorset, Miller says that asylum seekers can be detained indefinitely in the UK. Verne holds 580 individuals, 80% of whom receive no visitors, due in large part to its being effectively situated on an island miles from London, where most detainees' friends and family reside. Suicide rates are high. The centre also holds people who have been tortured in their home country, in violation of British law, but 'the Home Office frequently flouts its own rules'.[150]

Chapter 15

States and status

Article 15

(1) Everyone has the right to a nationality.

(2) No one shall be arbitrarily deprived of his nationality nor denied the right to change his nationality.

Statelessness usually occurs because people are born as refugees, live in countries where state boundaries change and/or are subject to ethnic and religious persecution. One third of stateless persons are children and a person becomes stateless every 10 minutes, according to the UN. As a former major colonial power, which once controlled countries with ongoing, chronic statelessness problems (including Malaysia and Sri Lanka), as well as being party to the UN Convention on the Reduction of Statelessness, the UK has a legal obligation to prevent individuals from being deprived of nationality.[151]

But in the UK *domestically*, persons are being stripped of their citizenship by the executive:

According to Home Office figures, since 1948 (when the Universal Declaration was adopted) and 1973 (when domestic powers fell into disuse), ten British citizens were made stateless after their citizenship was revoked. The powers to deprive individuals of citizenship were revived under the New Labour government with the adoption of the Nationality, Immigration and Asylum Act 2002. Between 2006 and early-2014, the Blair and subsequent Cameron governments had deprived 27 individuals of citizenship on the grounds of serving the broadly defined 'public good'.[152]

Returning to the issue of secret evidence and secret courts, the government refuses to say what percentage of those citizenship revocations were based on evidence presented in secret to the Home Office. One of the constraints on government power was protection within the Act against making a person stateless. However, the Tory-Liberal coalition soon remedied that. Between the years 2010 and 2015, Home Secretary and future PM Theresa May stripped 70 dual nationals of British citizenship without judicial review, often when they were visiting abroad; making their appeals impossible from countries such as Sudan and Pakistan.[153]

May's power was granted under the Immigration Act 2014. The Bureau of Investigative Journalists also notes that Home Secretary May's advisers slyly inserted the amendment into the Act which granted the Home Office the power to render individuals stateless. Even prior to the Act and its amendment being passed, '(t)wo of those who lost their citizenship' under Blair-era legislation, Mohamed Sakr and Bilal al Berjawi, 'went on to die in drone strikes, and a further man, Mahdi Hashi, was the subject of rendition to the US, where he was held in secret for over a month and now faces terror charges'.[154]

The arbitrary nature of the Act 'has relatively few international parallels', says David Anderson QC, who writes of the 'combination of those factors', in which 'deprivation of citizenship is exercisable on "conducive to the public good" grounds' and, crucially, '(the) fact that its exercise makes people stateless'. Anderson points out that the law contradicts the UN Convention on the Reduction of Statelessness 1961 and the Council of Europe's Convention on Nationality 1997. The European Network on Statelessness writes:

Britain has long been breaking ground in updating citizenship deprivation powers to the 21st century. Only now is it spreading, emulated...by Canada, and now tentatively by France in the wake of the November Paris attacks...Not only does Britain have the most developed legal deprivation powers among liberal democracies, it has also applied these powers much more liberally. Where most liberal democracies will go decades without issuing a single revocation, between 2006 and 2014 the British government served 27 deprivation orders on national security grounds alone.[155]

The think-tank Demos comments: 'With increasing frequency, the withdrawal of British citizenship is being used as a national security tool'. Author Louis Reynolds goes on to note that previous legislation enabled the executive to deny citizenship to persons suspected of potentially harming the 'public good', in some undefined way and in some undefined future. But with the 2014 legislation, and 'after a brief scuffle with the Lords(,) the Home Secretary has gained the power to make naturalised citizens stateless'.[156]

There are even moves to deprive persons born in the UK of citizenship. Syria's president Bashar al-Assad married a British-born Syrian, Asma. Proving their commitment to liberal principles, the Liberal Democrats wrote a formal letter to the Home Secretary, Amber Rudd, calling for Asma's citizenship to be revoked.[157]

Chapter 16

Right to marry?

Article 16

(1) Men and women of full age, without any limitation due to race, nationality or religion, have the right to marry and to found a family. They are entitled to equal rights as to marriage, during marriage and at its dissolution.

(2) Marriage shall be entered into only with the free and full consent of the intending spouses.

(3) The family is the natural and fundamental group unit of society and is entitled to protection by society and the State.

Damage to the family caused by socioeconomic factors has been documented in the introduction to this book. Turning to marriage specifically:

The year 2012 marked the centenary of Alan Turing's birth. Turing was a mathematician and early computer programmer whose work on encryption helped break the Nazis' Enigma Code. Turing's work helped Britain win the war. Because homosexuality was outlawed at the time, Turing was sentenced to chemical castration, which drove him to suicide. In 2009, New Labour's PM Gordon Brown issued an apology but refused to ask the queen for a formal pardon on behalf of Turing. To mark the centenary of Turing's birth, an online petition of over 23,000 signatures called for an official pardon. The Tory-Liberal government refused. Justice Minister Lord McNally (Liberal) who served Cameron's Tory government said: 'A posthumous pardon was not considered appropriate as Alan Turing was properly convicted of what at the time was a criminal offence'.[158]

The UK's Tory establishment remains deeply homophobic, as

its opposition to same-sex marriage reveals.

Homosexuality was outlawed in the UK until the passing of the Sexual Offences Act 1967. In 2004, the Gender Recognition Act passed into law. This meant that a person born in the physical body of, say, a male can be recognized as a female under domestic law. This meant that marriages had to be annulled because under British law until as late as 2013, a woman could only wed a man and vice versa. In 2011, Lynne Featherstone, the Liberal Under-Secretary for Equalities, launched a consultation which took place in 2012 concerning marriage rights for same-sex couples in England and Wales.[159]

The UK's state-sanctioned discrimination against homo-sexuals continued until as late 2013. Britain was slow to catch up with other European and several non-EU states. What follows are countries where same-sex marriage was legalized in chronological order: Netherlands 2001, Belgium 2003, Canada and Spain 2005, South Africa 2006, Norway and Sweden 2009, Argentina, Iceland and Portugal 2010, Denmark 2012, France, New Zealand and Uruguay 2013. Finally, the Marriages Act came into force in the UK in 2014, the same time that Estonia passed a law legalizing same-sex marriage.[160]

In 2013, a majority of Tories voted against the Marriage (Same Sex Couples) Act: 128 MPs against to 117 in favour. The bill made it into law because nearly every Labour MP voted in favour. The Act excludes Northern Ireland, where same-sex marriage remains illegal at the time of writing.[161]

The Tories got such bad press for their homophobia that at the end of the year, Tory Justice Minister Chris Grayling applied for a Royal Prerogative of Mercy, which was granted. In 2015, a petition signed by half a million Britons called for pardoning the estimated 49,000 men affected by homophobic legislation. Turing's great-niece Rachel Barnes told the BBC: 'We've always considered that it is totally unjust that only Alan was given a pardon'. In 2016, Scottish National Party MP, John

Nicolson, introduced the Sexual Offences (Pardons) Bill, dubbed the Turing law. The bill would have pardoned the thousands of men convicted under anti-sexuality laws in the UK, but the government blocked it.[162]

Instead, the ruling Tory party opted to amend the Policing and Crimes Bill to overturn convictions. The government praised itself and appropriated the name Turing law, after the Policing and Crime Bill received Royal Assent granting pardons for those who engaged in consensual same-sex relationships. According to the government website, however, 'this will only apply in cases where offenders have successfully applied through the Home Office's disregard process to have historic convictions removed'.

In 2017, PM Theresa May called a snap general election because the Labour Party opposition had not been so weak and divided since the 1980s. May claimed that the election was all about 'strengthening her hand' in Brussels over the Brexit negotiations. In reality, it was about guaranteeing another 5 years (7 in total since 2015) of Tory austerity. The plan backfired as May's approval rating sank, following a disastrous campaign. Record numbers of young voters backed her opponent, Jeremy Corbyn of the Labour Party; a party whose costed manifesto sought to equalize society, not further divide it. In the end, May's Tory government failed to get the 326 constituency seats needed for an outright majority. In order to reach the 326 number, May's team proposed forming a coalition government (which turned out to be a confidence-and-supply arrangement) with Northern Ireland's far-right Democratic Unionist Party (DUP).[163]

Northern Ireland's quasi-devolved parliament, the Northern Ireland Assembly Commission, represents 18 constituencies. In the UK general election 2017, the DUP won 10 seats. The DUP opposes fiscal austerity (unlike the Tories), but most of their other policies are regressive. Led by Protestant fanatics, the DUP openly opposes same-sex marriage and has campaigned against it.

Chapter 17

Home sweet home

Article 17

(1) Everyone has the right to own property alone as well as in association with others.

(2) No one shall be arbitrarily deprived of his property.

According to YouGov, 80% of renters would like to own their home, but 41% think they never will. Campbell Robb, chief executive of the charity Shelter, says: 'Everyone should have the chance of a stable future where they can put down roots, but for many the reality is a lifetime of frustration that they can't move on in life, coping with expensive and unstable private renting, and feeling alienated'.[164]

In the neoliberal economy, housing is a commodity not a human right. Successive British governments have refused to sufficiently regulate the housing market and in doing so violate Article 17. The class-conscious system favours landlords over tenants and private ownership over affordable, long-term state-owned housing. It also has damaging effects on social progress, as most older people vote Tory and own their homes. Tories rely heavily on home-owners for votes. In addition, Tories are more tempted to sell off social housing to get a few more prospective voters onto the property ladder and in doing so inflate prices even further.

A restricted report for the Treasury (2002-03) obtained under the Freedom of Information Act reveals that:

(t)he UK housing market has in the past been a source of instability...This occurred most recently in the late 1980s when the combination of loose monetary and fiscal policy and a housing boom led to RPIX (the housing index) inflation above 10%, interest rates at 15%, 1.5m families with negative equity and a consumption-driven recession.[165]

The report predated the financial crisis (which was triggered by the US subprime mortgage bubble) by 5 to 6 years. It goes on to note that 'house prices (in the UK) have been rising at unsustainable rates relative to income growth'. In 1993, the percentage of first-time buyers was 46. By 2003, it was 28%. '(M)- any potential buyers are being priced out of the market', the report continues. One of the results is that under-35s 'remain within their parents' household for longer than desired'.[166]

It is worth remembering that the report was written when New Labour's Tony Blair was PM and Gordon Brown his chancellor. New Labour introduced undergraduate fees and increased postgraduate fees. The housing report cites student debt as a factor in the unaffordability of first-time properties for young people. Luckily for the banks and other lenders, this did not lead to market 'cooling' because landlords were 'enter(ing) the market for long-term rental income'. The more properties bought up by speculators, the more demand for physical houses and higher the prices.[167]

The for-profit, class-based housing system (including regulations and tax breaks) laid the basis for the current crisis, in which millions of Britons will never own a home. The Office for National Statistics notes that average earnings grew 68% between 1997 and 2016. Property prices in the same period rose 259%, meaning that working people spent 7.6 times their yearly earnings on buying a home in England and Wales, compared to 3.6 in 1997. The *Financial Times* notes that '(t)he rise in house prices has helped to reverse a century of rising home ownership and driven an increase in private renting'.[168]

The annual housing survey notes that by 2017, home ownership in the UK had fallen to its lowest level since 1985.

Lindsay Judge of the Resolution Foundation says: 'More than double the share of families live in the private rented sector today than did in 1992'. However, the Resolution Foundation notes that when complexities in the housing market are factored into equations (such as 'single-owner' properties housing lodgers, and 'families' including single parents with one or more children), the statistics are even bleaker. Just 51% of owners occupy homes.[169]

Britain's housing crisis has devastating effects on health. Thirty-six per cent of Britons rent (19% of whom rent privately, 17% rent social housing). More than 35% of tenants experience anxiety or depression at least once within 12 months, compared to 21% of owners. The activist group Generation Rent, which commissioned the Survation poll, comments: 'Private renters are typically in short, insecure tenancies, which makes life unstable and household finances unpredictable. Social tenants are more likely to be under financial pressure from reforms to social security'.[170]

High house prices have adverse effects on fertility and infant health. The European Bank for Reconstruction and Development finds that among owners, an increase in housing costs of 10% leads to a fall in birth rates of 1.3%, as couples delay starting a family until they can afford to buy outright or earn better salaries. However, for renters, an increase in costs of 2.8% leads to a decline in birth rates of 4.9%. It is well known that the later one has a child, the more the health risks to mother and baby. Falling fertility in Europe is also increasing immigration, as employers look to foreigners to fill skills shortages. According to the charity Shelter, those who are too poor to ever make it onto the property ladder will end their lives £561,000 poorer than their property-owning counterparts; for London, the figure is £1.36 million. Lifers in the rental sector, according to Shelter, run an increased risk of relationship instability and social alienation, as friends buy and can end up shifting loyalties to the middle-class.[171]

Chapter 18

Thought crimes

Article 18

Everyone has the right to freedom of thought, conscience and religion; this right includes freedom to change his religion or belief, and freedom, either alone or in community with others and in public or private, to manifest his religion or belief in teaching, practice, worship and observance.

Social media, Facebook, Twitter, Instagram, YouTube, has become so much a part of most Britons' everyday lives that it is an extension of thought. Before social media, people kept their opinions to themselves, friends, family, colleagues and, if something was a burning issue, wrote letters to local or national newspapers. Phone-in radio shows were also an outlet for expressing thoughts and exchanging ideas. If an individual really wanted large numbers of people to pay attention to them, they would self-publish (books or pamphlets) or even stand on street corners and preach.

The digital age has made thought expression so easy as to tempt users into publishing their thoughts at the click of a button. Perhaps more importantly, friends, family and colleagues now *expect* us to communicate through social media. For better or worse, millions of social media users feel compelled to update their pages with moment-to-moment thoughts and trivia. Social media is contradictory. It is both narcissistic and fulfilling a need to belong to a community.

For years now, the British government has monitored social media and made mass arrests of jokers, idiots, mentally ill persons and those who snap or get drunk and post threatening messages. Since the passing of the Communications Act 2003 by the New Labour government, strict limits have been placed on freedom of thought. Section 127 is worth reading at length, as it demonstrates the broad criteria for committing a criminal 'offence' on social media. The legislation defines 'offence' in such broad terms as to give law enforcement an excuse to arrest anyone the government deems a political threat or a threat to 'values', such as blanket support for the Armed Forces or secular-democratic customs. This directly threatens Article 18 of the Universal Declaration in that it inhibits individuals from freely expressing their thoughts.

Section 127 of the Communications Act 2003 states:

Improper use of public electronic communications network
(1) A person is guilty of an offence if he—
(a) sends by means of a public electronic communications network a message or other matter that is grossly offensive or of an indecent, obscene or menacing character; or
(b) causes any such message or matter to be so sent.
(2) A person is guilty of an offence if, for the purpose of causing annoyance, inconvenience or needless anxiety to another, he—
(a) sends by means of a public electronic communications network, a message that he knows to be false,
(b) causes such a message to be sent; or
(c) persistently makes use of a public electronic communications network.[172]

A Freedom of Information request published by Gareth Corfield of *The Register* reveals that between 2010 and 2015, 2,500 Londoners were arrested by the Metropolitan Police under Section 127 of the Communications Act. Their 'crimes' included posting 'offensive' or 'annoying' comments or images on social media.[173]

The year 2012 was a trying one for freedom of expression.

Matthew Woods (19) was imprisoned for three months after posting sexual jokes about children who had been abducted in real-life. Azhar Ahmed was prosecuted for writing on Facebook (his errors uncorrected):[174]

> People gassin about deaths of Soldiers! What about the innocent familys who have been brutally killed.. The women who have been raped.. The children who have been sliced up..! Your enemy's were the Taliban not innocent harmful (sic—harmless) familys. All soldiers should DIE & go to HELL! THE LOWLIFE FOKKIN SCUM! gotta problem go cry at your soldiers grave and wish him hell because thats where he is going.. (sic) (ellipses and emphases in original).[175]

Interestingly, Ahmed was arrested on suspicion of committing a 'racially aggravated public order offence'. The Index on Censorship (IoC) was critical of the arrest, writing: 'Unconditional support for soldiers is now expected, even as we become increasingly unsure of what they're doing out there (on the battlefield)'. The IoC concludes: 'From the most ardent supporter of the war to the most strident critic, everyone claims to be acting in the interest of Our Brave Boys. This is now not a matter of politics, but loyalty'.[176]

Also in 2012, 19-year-old Linney House posted on Facebook an image of himself burning a poppy on Remembrance Sunday. He wrote: 'How about that you squadey cunts' (sic). After House was identified by the far-right English Defence League (whose members have made their fair share of offensive anti-Muslim statements), he was arrested within hours under the Malicious Communications Act 1988 and had his phone seized. House faced a media naming and shaming, but the charges were dropped. One wonders if the armed forces will apologize for burning human beings to death with Hellfire missiles launched from Predator drones?[177]

In 2014, Ann Maguire, a teacher in Leeds, was stabbed to death by a pupil. Former pupil Jake Newsome (21) wrote on Facebook (mistakes uncorrected): 'im glad that teacher got stabbed up, feel sorry for the kid (who did it) ... he shoulda pissed on her too'. Newsome was arrested and charged under the Communications Act and jailed for six weeks. Forty-two-year-old Robert Riley was arrested and imprisoned for eight weeks for tweeting that he would have liked to kill Maguire and her colleagues.[178]

Once, we would have ignored, challenged or tried to educate people who made racist and offensive remarks. Now the state has made an industry of monitoring, arresting, fining and/or imprisoning them.

Chapter 19

Freedom...within limits

Article 19

Everyone has the right to freedom of opinion and expression; this right includes freedom to hold opinions without interference and to seek, receive and impart information and ideas through any media and regardless of frontiers.

The word libel strikes fear into the hearts of publishers and broadcasters.

After Britons were driven into the industrial towns and cities by land closure acts and periodic food crises in previous centuries, living standards declined. Chartism and other political movements laid the basis for representative democracy in the UK, which came as late as the turn of the twentieth century, with the right to vote being gradually yielded to working class men. One of the weapons used by lords, the church and monarchy against working-class progress in the area of political representation was so-called sedition, defamation and libel.

For centuries, Britain has been ruled by unusually severe libel laws which restrict freedom of expression and opinion, particularly through media channels: print, radio and television. If an individual writes or records something that someone doesn't like, both author and publisher/broadcaster can be sued for defamation (libel). What makes the UK a particularly acute case is the fact that common law – presumption of innocence – does not apply in libel cases. In British libel cases, the accused must prove their innocence. This has led to law firms engaging in 'libel tourism', suing for easy money.

Even worse, vital information about criminals working in business and government is often kept from the public.

Corporations, for instance, can potentially get away with crimes by slamming an investigation by journalists into those crimes as libel.

In 2006, scholars Robert O. Collins and J. Millard Burr published *Alms for Jihad*, in which they allege that the late billionaire banker Khalid bin Mahfouz (who died in 2009) funded international terrorism from his native Saudi Arabia, a claim denied by Mahfouz and his family. Cambridge University Press avoided a libel case brought by Mahfouz by destroying all unsold print copies and apologizing to Mahfouz.[179]

In 2008, the UN Committee on Human Rights wrote that British libel laws 'discourage critical media reporting on matters of serious public interest, adversely affecting the ability of scholars and journalists to publish their work, including through the phenomenon known as libel tourism'. One example of the latter is the case of Dr Rachel Ehrenfeld, who was sued by Mahfouz and his sons for writing a book, *Funding Evil*, which sold fewer than 30 copies in the UK. Ehrenfeld, who is American, is protected in her native country under First Amendment provisions; but not in the UK. The most appalling aspect of the case is the fact that Ehrenfeld's book was never published in the UK. The online sales meant that Mahfouz could file his libel claim against her in Britain. The *New York Times* reported: 'In the Internet age, almost every American book can be bought in Britain. That means American authors are subject to being sued under British libel law'.[180]

The Defamation Act 2013 was supposedly adopted in an effort to reform the much-criticized libel laws. In reality, the Defamation Act 2013 makes stating a fact a possible civil offence and stating an opinion a defence. Article 3 sections 1 and 2 state:

(1) It is a defence to an action for defamation for the defendant to show that the

(2) ...statement complained of was a statement of opinion.[181]

NOTHING ON TV

It's not just libel narrowing the knowledge of the British public. After the *Guardian* published reports leaked by Edward Snowden concerning government surveillance and war crimes, the newspapers' journalists were threatened. The UN Special Rapporteur on Freedom of Expression stated: 'I have been absolutely shocked about the way the *Guardian* has been treated, from the idea of prosecution to the fact that some members of parliament even called it treason...I think that is unacceptable in a democratic society'.[182]

In addition to arresting and intimidating journalists, the government has on several occasions outlawed foreign news services from broadcasting in the UK via satellite.

Kurds are people peculiarly affected by colonialism. When the West imposed its nation-state system on the world in the days of empire, artificial boundaries were imposed on peoples, many of whom to this day rejected them; for instance, the Pashtuns, who were caught between the British-created border between Afghanistan and India (now Pakistan). Kurds ended up having no state as a people. There are significant populations of Kurds in Turkey, Iraq (in the semi-autonomous Kurdistan) and Syria. One of the many political organizations claiming to represent them, the PKK, has engaged in terrorism against Turkey. Turkey has a long history of appalling violence against Kurdish civilians in the 1980s and 90s, with violence picking up again in more recent years. Thousands of Kurdish civilians have been killed and tens of thousands driven from their homes with US, British and German weapons and training. The Kurds of Iraq were exterminated in large numbers by Saddam Hussein during the *Anfal* genocide, which was also backed by the US and Britain.[183]

Until it was replaced in 2003, the UK's Independent Television Commission issued and revoked licences to broadcasters. In the mid-1990s, the six-language, London-based MED TV was issued with a licence to broadcast from the UK. Under the pretext that the channel was likely to 'incite people to violence', the ITC revoked the licence, depriving Britons and Europeans of the chance to learn about the suffering of Kurds during Turkey's persecution; and more importantly the role their governments play in atrocities.[184]

Turning to Iran: In 2011, the US and Britain imposed illegal sanctions on the country over its refusal to bend to US pressure over its legal, civilian nuclear energy programme, which the US does not want Iran to develop. The sanctions are illegal under Article 33 of the IV Geneva Convention. The UN reported that rising food and particularly medicine prices caused by the sanctions were seriously harming the public. Then-Defence Secretary Philip Hammond told the media that the aim of the sanctions was to hurt the public to the point that they put pressure on their government to bend to US demands. Hammond added: 'We can definitely make the pain much greater'.[185]

Shortly after the UK's imposition of sanctions, OFCOM (which replaced the ITC in 2003) revoked the licence of Iran's Press TV. The alleged reason for the ban was the alleged mistreatment of journalist Maziar Bahari. Back in 2009, Bahari (who worked for *Newsweek*) said that he was threatened with execution by captors in Tehran (Iran's capital) to report a pro-government story. Press TV refused to pay OFCOM's £100,000 fine and lost its licence in 2012, conveniently timed to hide the impact of UK-backed sanctions on Iran from the British public, who might have otherwise learned about them and pressured the government to stop hurting innocent Iranians.[186]

From 1990-2003, the UK killed 200,000 Iraqis (to cite a low-end estimate by the British House of Commons Library) by launching a blockade on Iraqi medicine, sanitation chemicals and surgical equipment. The UN and other agencies put the death toll at 1 million; mostly of children under five. Apart from John Pilger's single documentary, *Paying the Price* (2000), media censorship and lack of interest meant that the sanctions ran for 13 years with minimal protest from Britons.[187]

Chapter 20

Right to protest

Article 20

(1) Everyone has the right to freedom of peaceful assembly and association.

(2) No one may be compelled to belong to an association.

The government has numerous ways of blocking peaceful protest in the UK: prohibition, privatization of land, infiltration of protest groups, intimidation and use of so-called less-than-lethal weapons, like tear gas.

In the case of prohibition: The New Labour government adopted the Serious Organised Crime and Police Act 2005, which introduced the Serious Organised Crime Police Agency, or Britain's FBI as many called it. Tucked away in the 276-page legislation is a ban on protesting within 1 kilometre of the Houses of Parliament. The ban was imposed due to the relentless struggles of anti-war protestor Brian Haw, who died in 2011. Haw set up a camp outside Parliament, where he and some supporters had stayed since 2001, following the bombing of Afghanistan by Britain and the US. Haw became an embarrassment to Parliament as his presence alerted visitors to the crimes of most of those dwelling within.[188]

The Tory-Liberal-imposed Police Reform and Social Responsibility Act 2011 went even further, prohibiting a number of activities for up to 90 days in Parliament Square, including operating noisy equipment (for example, loudhailers), erecting tents and laying sleeping bags. It is worth noting that the Act came into force after the Occupy London protests of 2010, which were provoked by the government's response to the financial crisis, namely imposing austerity on the public while giving hand-outs to the rich.[189]

With regards to private land: The human rights group Liberty, together with the National Union of Students, notes

> Private bodies, whether companies or individuals, are not required by the Human Rights Act to act compatibly with rights protected by the European Convention on Human Rights, so a refusal to allow a protest on privately owned land cannot be challenged directly under the Human Rights Act. With many parts of our cities and towns now in private ownership (e.g. Canary Wharf in London, Liverpool One in Liverpool) this is increasingly a problem.[190]

GET IN THERE!

With regards to infiltration: Britain's domestic subversion units, MI5 and Special Branch, have long histories of infiltrating and monitoring protest groups, most notoriously the latter's Special Demonstration Squad. In more recent years, reporters Evans and Lewis wrote a long exposé of police infiltration into non-violent protest groups, including the use of police provocateurs, some of whom encouraged animal rights groups to commit domestic terrorism (for example, bombing a shop while it was closed) to discredit and eventually lead to the outlawing of the given groups.[191]

According to its website, the National Extremism Tactical Coordination Unit promotes 'a coordinated response to domestic extremism by providing tactical advice to the police service, and information and guidance to industry and government'. One such group of extremists was featured on the agency's website to illustrate the threat Britons face every day: from clowns. Undercover cop Lynn Watson (not her real name) painted red dots on her cheeks to penetrate the Leeds-based Clandestine Insurgent Rebel Clown Army. The group used humour to draw public attention to atrocities committed in Iraq by the British and

Americans, staging a mock invasion and liberation of Leeds.[192]

Turning to intimidation: For large demonstrations, police often use a technique of containment (usually called kettling). This involves temporarily imprisoning protestors in a street or square using cordons, including horses and barricades. In 2009, to take one particularly controversial example, 10,000 people protested in London against the Group of 20 meeting being held in the city. Police efforts to contain protestors provoked violent responses from those who tried to break free.[193]

In 2013, at the invitation of the British government, the UN Rapporteur on the Right to Freedom of Peaceful Assembly and Association, Maina Kiai, visited the UK and authored a report. Kiai stated:

> I am deeply concerned with the use of embedded undercover police officers in groups that are non-violent and which exercise their democratic rights to protest and take peaceful direct action...The case of Mark Kennedy and other undercover officers is shocking as the groups in question were not engaged in criminal activities. The duration of this infiltration, and the resultant trauma and suspicion it has caused, are unacceptable in a democracy. It is a clear violation of basic rights protected under the Human Rights Act, and more generally under international law, such as the right to privacy.

Kiai went on to talk about surveillance and kettling:

> I am further concerned about the police practice of containment or 'kettling' which has been used in London in the past years. I take note of a number of decisions by British courts which ruled in favour of the practice, and which have recently been confirmed by the European Court of Human Rights.
>
> Nevertheless, I believe that this practice is detrimental to

the exercise of the right to freedom of peaceful assembly due to its indiscriminate and disproportionate nature.

I heard, for instance, appalling stories of peaceful protestors, as well as innocent by-standers - such as tourists - held for long hours with no access to water or sanitary facilities. It also undeniably has a powerful chilling effect on the exercise of freedom of peaceful assembly, and I was informed of many people who refrained from exercising their right to freedom of peaceful assembly for fear of being kettled. Finally, it appears that kettling is used for intelligence gathering purposes, by compelling those kettled to disclose their name and address as they leave the kettle, increasing the chilling effect it has on potential protesters.[194]

Finally, the use of weapons: For decades, the British government has allowed police to attack domestic demonstrators with numerous so-called less-than-lethal weapons, including tear gas, tasers and rubber bullets. As noted in Chapter 6, tasers amount to torture.

Chapter 21

Democracy

Article 21

(1) Everyone has the right to take part in the government of his country, directly or through freely chosen representatives.

(2) Everyone has the right of equal access to public service in his country.

(3) The will of the people shall be the basis of the authority of government; this will shall be expressed in periodic and genuine elections which shall be by universal and equal suffrage and shall be held by secret vote or by equivalent free voting procedures.

Britain is not a democracy. It is a constitutional monarchy. But the 'constitution' is a fable. Unlike most countries, Britain has no *written* constitution. It is therefore a monarchy. Each elected government and Prime Minister is approved by the monarch. Any law can be overturned by the Royal Prerogative (as we saw in Chapter 1). Britain is part theocracy. The monarch pledges to serve 'god' in their coronation speeches, not the people. The unelected House of Lords is divided into the Lords Temporal and the Lords Spiritual. How many other so-called advanced democracies have an unelected clergy in their parliaments? Britain's democratic procedures are based on a host of traditions and laws.[195]

The City of London Corporation is a state within a state. It has its own parliament and police force (the Metropolitan Police).[196]

Britain's local councilors are hamstrung by the centralization of power, which means that a Tory government, for example, can and does selectively defund Labour or Liberal Democrat-run councils. Also, the incumbent government can and does pass laws to help itself cling to power: fixed-term parliaments, the right to call an election early (essentially giving a strong government additional time in power) and constituency boundary changes which can win the party more voters. Britain's electoral system for national elections is called a first past-the-post system. Britain's 650 constituencies (at the time of writing) are uneven in terms of numbers of constituents. In wealthy areas (that is, areas with a higher density of Tory voters), there are more constituencies (giving the Tories greater representation). This results in highly disproportional parliamentary seat shares.[197]

In the 2017 general election, the Tories won 43% of the vote and ended up with 318 seats. Labour came very close in terms of vote share, with 40%, but won only 262 seats. The Liberal Democrats got 7.39% of the votes but only 1.85% of the seats. This translates as 12 Liberal Democrat seats in Parliament. The Scottish National Party got 5.38% of the votes or 3.04% of the seats in Parliament, yet this translates as 35 seats.[198]

There are many different types of proportional representation. In one particular system analyzed by the left-leaning *Independent*, the Tories would have won just 276 seats. Labour would have lost a seat and achieved 261 seats. The Lib Dems would have won 48. UKIP, which won no seats, would have won 12 and the Greens, which won a single seat, would have won 11. The Scottish National Party would have won only 20; Plaid Cymru would have lost a seat (they won 4) and the far-right Democratic Unionist Party of Northern Ireland would have won only 6 (they won 10). Their rival Sinn Féin would have won 5 seats (they won 7).[199]

These results show that while many parties would lose seats, the Tories would lose by far the most, paving the way for the formation of progressive alliances and progressive-centrist coalitions. In conclusion, the system is skewed in favour of the Tories.

RANK AND OPINION

In a 2011 study of 30 democracies in the so-called developed world, Britain ranked 26, ahead of Costa Rica, South Arica, Poland and France. The best democracies, according to the research, are Denmark, Finland, Belgium and Iceland. Zurich University's Democracy Barometer has 12 measures to determine the 'quality of democracy'. They are: freedom, individual liberties, rule of law, public sphere, control, competition, mutual constraints, governmental capability, equality, transparency, participation and representation.[200]

Public dissatisfaction with British democracy is reflected in other measures. Trust in politicians remains low. The more trusted professions are doctors (trusted by 89% of Britons), teachers (86%) and judges (80%). The following professionals are the least trusted: journalists (25%), estate agents (25%), government ministers (22%) and 'politicians generally' (21%). 'This question has been asked consistently since 1983, making it the longest-running series on trust in key professions in the UK', said the researchers. 'It shows that public trust in politicians has always been low: at no point since 1983 have more than a quarter of the public ever trusted politicians to tell the truth'. The police are trusted by nearly seven in ten Britons, as are clergy. The implication is that most Britons would trust a theocratic police-state more than the present so-called democracy.[201]

A 2012 survey by YouGov finds the high percentage of Britons who agree that we live in a democracy 'deceptively reassuring'. When probed further, the following percentages of Britons agreed that Parliament 'understands the daily lives of people like you', 12%; 'represents the interests and wishes of people like you', 15%; 'reflects the full range of people and views of the British electorate', 16%; and 'debates issues of public concern in a sensible and considered way', 24% (sic). Nearly six in ten Britons (58%) agreed that '(i)t doesn't make a difference to my daily life who wins general elections...there's very little real difference between the main political parties'.[202]

The survey also reveals that most Britons (71%) think that local MPs should 'make a great deal of difference' to daily lives; but only 29% think they do in practice. In addition, 75% agreed that councilors should make a difference, but only 58% believed they did. When people were asked who has the most influence, the following said government (85%), banks and financial institutions (79%), the EU (74%) and big business (71%). Interestingly, 87% agreed that government should have an influence, but only 16% agreed that banks and financial institutions should have such influence, as did 24% who thought that the EU and big business should help to run the show. The outlook gets even more dire. Just 4% agreed that politicians pay most attention to voters in their constituency, but 64% agreed that they should.[203]

Aside from too much centralization of power, public frustration with democracy is worsened by the refusal of successive governments to implement policies which reflect the public's wishes on a host of issues. Depending on the war in question, a plurality-to-majority of Britons oppose war, yet the government consistently attacks other countries unlawfully. A huge majority, even of Tory voters (68%), agree that foreign wars enhance the risk of terrorism at home, despite successive government's repeated efforts to deny the obvious after attacks on British territory.[204]

A YouGov poll in 2017 suggests that a majority of Britons want most services placed in the public sector. Percentages in favour versus against: police 87% versus 3%, the NHS 84% versus 10%, Armed Forces 83% versus 3%, schools 81% versus 6%, Royal Mail 65% versus 21%, railway companies 60% versus 25%, water 59% versus 25%, BBC 58% versus 25%, energy companies 53% versus 31% and bus companies 50% versus 35%. The remaining percentages didn't know. A majority of the remaining respondents felt that telephone and internet providers, banks and airlines should remain in the private sector.[205]

Chapter 22

The war on benefits

Article 22

Everyone, as a member of society, has the right to social security and is entitled to realization, through national effort and international co-operation and in accordance with the organization and resources of each State, of the economic, social and cultural rights indispensable for his dignity and the free development of his personality.

Business lobbies for austerity with devastating results. If governments introduce a fiscal stimulus to help recover from an economic crisis, they could levy heavier taxes on the rich to pay for it. In an effort to pre-empt this, the rich lobby for austerity which hurts easy targets: the rest of the population.

The effects have been deadly. According to government figures released under the Freedom of Information Act (following a battle with the Department for Work and Pensions and the Information Officer who is responsible for investigating FOIA refusals), 2,380 people died between December 2011 and February 2014 when their claims for Employment Support Allowance ended after failing Work Capability Assessments. These assessments were run by private companies contracted to get as many people off benefits as possible. The DWP figures include people who died in poverty, committed suicide, whose refrigerated medication went bad following electricity cuts due to late payments, and stress-related heart-attacks.[206]

It is hardly surprising that the United Nations Committee on Economic, Social and Cultural Rights condemned the UK over its cuts in 2016. 'The Committee is particularly concerned about the adverse impact of (benefit) changes and cuts on the enjoyment of the rights to social security and to an adequate standard of living by disadvantaged and marginalized individuals and groups'. It lists 'women, children, persons with disabilities, low-income families and families with two or more children' as major victims. 'The Committee also is concerned about the extent to which the State party has made use of sanctions in relation to social security benefits and the absence of due process and access to justice for those affected by the use of sanctions'.[207]

The worst part is that the government/tabloid-TV assaults on benefit claimants have been successful. A majority of Britons, having lost some or much of their wealth after the crash of 2008, backed the attack on benefits. The harsher the Tory policy, the higher the party's approval rating. According to a 2011 YouGov poll, 73% of respondents supported 'making the long term unemployed do compulsory work...or risk losing benefits'. A further 66% thought that people who refuse to do the first job that comes along should lose their benefits. Even with regards to people on Disability Living Allowance, 69% backed tougher assessments. Sixty-eight per cent supported capping housing benefit, even if it meant people had to move house.[208]

BAD NEWS

The amount of political, tabloid and TV-based lying about social security is one of the most impressive achievements of the British propaganda system. According to Strathclyde University and the Glasgow University Media Group, print articles focusing on disability and fraud increased from 2.8% in 2005/06 to 6.1% in 2010/11, coinciding with the new Tory-Liberal coalition and their austerity agenda. A study by the University of Kent states: 'Our analysis of media coverage of benefits in national newspapers from 1995 to 2011 found that while newspapers contain both positive and negative representations of claimants, the content of press stories is indeed skewed towards negative representations'. It concludes that 'both the language and content of "negative" coverage have changed substantially over time. While (alleged benefit) fraud remains very important in negative coverage, articles are much more likely now to refer to lack of reciprocity and effort on the part of claimants than they were previously'.[209]

The general message is that disabled people are faking (reinforced by TV shows which claim to catch fraudsters), foreigners come here to scrounge because of our liberal attitudes toward hand-outs (welfare tourism), lazy people can't be bothered to work (benefits as a 'lifestyle choice' according to PM Cameron) and levels of fraud among the able-bodied are high.

Most Britons have a false perception of social security. Most think that 30% of claimants are fraudsters, when in reality fewer than 1% of benefit claimants engage in fraud and/or are overpaid due to government clerical errors. Most Britons think that their taxes go to lazy scroungers, when in fact 1.1% of social security spending goes to the unemployed. By far the biggest chunk goes to retired persons: 46.43%. Next comes disabled people (19.28%). After the disabled come tax credit claimants (working and child, total 13.06%). Next come people who already work and need extra money for housing (rents too high) and income support (pay too low, 12.82% in total). After those claimants come child benefit recipients, including pay for single parents, maternity leave and Sure Starts grants etc. (6.71%). The rest is spent on universal credit, the Christmas bonus and bereavement benefits.[210]

CAPPING THE POOR

In 2011, the government legislated to cap benefit payments for properties of different sizes. Persons living in one-bedroom properties were capped at £250 per week, two bedrooms £290 per week, three bedrooms £340 and four bedrooms £400. These cuts mostly affected Londoners, where housing costs are notoriously harsh. The government estimated that 160,000 households would be affected, with 17,500 losing on average £81 per week.[211]

In the same year, they also introduced widely-criticized Work Capability Assessments (WCAs), which targeted 1.5 million claimants with disabilities. Failed applicants lost their incapacity benefits (replaced with Employment Support Allowance) and were forced to apply for Job Seekers' Allowance, even though many were disabled. The government's own figures suggest that of the 40% of appealed cases, 38% were successful. This implies that many WCA outcomes were contrary to British law.[212]

Until 2011, social security rates were fixed to the Retail Price Index. But Chancellor Osborne adjusted it according to the Consumer Price Index. Because the latter rises slower than the former, the adjustment amounted to a long-term reduction in benefits by an average of £10 per week, which is significant considering the cost of food in the UK, hence the reliance of 1 million Britons on food banks.[213]

In 2012, Disability Living Allowance (which accompanied incapacity benefits) was replaced with Personal Independence Payment (PIP). A non-means-tested benefit, PIPs wiped a further £100 million from disabled people's benefits. The government estimated that half a million people would lose their benefits under the new scheme.[214]

In 2013, the Bank of England estimated that inflation would rise by 2.3%. The government announced a benefits and tax credit increase of 1%, meaning a decrease in social security of 1.3%. The 2013 cap for out-of-work families (most of whom live in London, one of Europe's most expensive cities) was set at £500 per week, even for large families. According to the government's own figures, this affected 56,000 families who lost an average £93 per week. A benefit cap introduced in that year targeted those in receipt of housing benefit or universal credit, where the household is not entitled to tax credits. Where the household's income from Income Support, Jobseekers' Allowance or Employment Support Allowance exceeds the cap, other benefits are reduced. A year later, the government imposed a spending cap on social security, down from £200,000 million per annum to £114,900 million by 2021.[215]

Also in 2013, the government introduced under-occupancy legislation, referred to as 'bedroom tax', which disproportion-ately affected disabled persons for a variety of reasons, such as: siblings or a parent left home; the extra room stores medi-cal equipment; the property is otherwise suitable for their needs (for example, it has a bedroom on the ground floor), it was the only property the family could find or afford at the time and so on. As noted, this particularly cruel tax was condemned by the UN. Benefits were deducted by 14% per week for persons with one 'excess' bedroom and 25% for those with two or more bed-rooms.[216]

In early-2014, long before it had an agenda to bash the UK over Brexit, the European Committee on Social Rights found that in real terms, the UK's social security spending was below the European average and that Article 12 of the European Social Charter was thus being violated. It labelled as 'manifestly inadequate' incapacity benefits (which the government then dismantled altogether), 'state pensions and job seekers (benefits)'. It also exploded the benefit tourism myth, stating that most migrants work and few claim benefits.[217]

In 2016, housing benefit for single claimants was capped at £257.69, down £296.35; except for London claimants.[218]

The fact is that people on benefits are an easy target. Most are hardworking (no time to organize and not usually represented by unions), poor (not enough money to take legal action against cuts or sanctions) and/or are very socially divided (often disabled, ethnic minorities, single mothers). As candidate Cameron told the TV media prior to the general election in 2010: 'We're going to hit hardest those on incapacity benefit'; in other words, hit hardest those who can't hit back.

Chapter 23

Exploiting workers, crushing unions

Article 23

(1) Everyone has the right to work, to free choice of employment, to just and favourable conditions of work and to protection against unemployment.

(2) Everyone, without any discrimination, has the right to equal pay for equal work.

(3) Everyone who works has the right to just and favourable remuneration ensuring for himself and his family an existence worthy of human dignity, and supplemented, if necessary, by other means of social protection.

(4) Everyone has the right to form and to join trade unions for the protection of his interests.

At the time of writing, the UK has refused to ratify several conventions of the UN's International Labour Organization: Night Work (Women) 1919 ('(d)enounced on 25 January 1937'); Night Work of Young Persons (Industry) ('(d)enounced on 04 Oct 1947)'; Workmen's Compensation (Occupational Diseases) 1925 ('(d)enounced on 29 April 1936'); Inspection of Emigrants 1926; Minimum Wage-Fixing Machinery ('(d)enounced on 25 July 1985'); Underground Work (Women) 1935 ('(d)enounced on May 26 May 1988'); and so on.[219]

Despite the above, the UK has ratified most ILO conventions. However, referring to three specific conventions, legal specialist Chris Syder writes that '(w)hen the UK government ratified these ILO conventions (in 1949, 1950 and 1980 respectively) it agreed to put in place national laws and practices that comply with the convention provisions'. Syder concludes, however, that 'the Experts do not have a judicial mandate so their evaluation of the UK's national industrial relations legislation and practices carry no judicial force'.[220]

The Tory government likes to boast that record numbers of people are in work, but as Bart Cammaerts of the London School of Economics notes, 1.8 million of those 'employed' are on so-called zero-hours contracts, which are 'inherently exploitative'. This is due in large measure to the weakness of unions, he says; the real reasons for union weakness are documented below. Zero-hours amount to 'post-modern slavery', he continues: 34% of contracts are awarded to 16 to 24-year-olds.[221]

In 2012, PM Cameron told the Tory conference that the government's mandatory work scheme would intensify with changes to entitlements and commitments on behalf of claimants to find work; however unsuitable for them. Cameron said that under the new rules, 'you have to seek work and take work or you will lose your benefit'. One of the consequences of this policy was so-called workfare, which imposed 'sanctions' on claimants if they refused to work for free in order to continue claiming their meagre entitlements. In the first few months of its imposition, claims for jobseekers' allowance dropped by 46%. Of those who continued to claim and who ended up in workfare positions, many were exploited by some of the 500+ companies, including charities, which won contracts with the government to use the forced labour of claimants. Some of the bigger companies using workfare victims include ASDA, Bernardo's (ironically, a children's charity), BHF, Boots, the Co-op (ironically, a 'worker-owned' store), DHL, Matalan, Nando's, Oxfam, Pound Stretcher, Sue Ryder and, of course, Tesco. These companies deny any wrongdoing.[222]

Aidan McQuade of Anti-Slavery said: 'I think the workfare programme can (constitute) forced labour. Forced labour's defined in international law as being all work or service exacted from a person under menace of any sort of penalty, for which they haven't offered themselves voluntarily. I think some of the manifestations that we've seen of the workfare programme suggest that it is forced labour'.[223]

UNION DECLINE

Finally, turning to unions:

'In most continental European countries, collective agreements have the force of a legal contract', so says an OECD report from the early-1990s concerning the legal power of unions and collective bargaining in Europe. 'By contrast, in British law a collective agreement is no more than a gentleman's agreement, a compromise for as long as neither of the parties wants to withdraw from it'. Between 1990 and 1998, the John Major Tory government and the start of the New Labour Blair government, union membership declined from 9.9 million to 7.8 million, including in the public and private sectors.[224]

In 2013, Maina Kiai, UN Special Rapporteur on the Rights to Freedom of Peaceful Assembly and of Association, analysed the UK. He documented 'undue constraints on the right to strike', an 'issue...criticized by the International Labour Organisation on repeated occasions. It is time to repeal this law and bring the UK into conformity with human rights law'. Kiai concluded: 'I was appalled to hear about the existence of a blacklist of union members in the construction industry, with no sanctions allegedly taken against those who benefitted from the list. It is crucial that strong actions be taken against the making and using of such lists as a deterrence'. Nothing was done, following an Early Day Motion (986) tabled by Labour's John McDonnell, which failed to gain traction in a Tory-led Parliament with a largely right-wing Labour Party coming second.[225]

The same standards are not applied to the democratic procedures and criteria of government as to unions and the latter's legal ability to strike. An article from 2015 by John Hendy QC is worth quoting at length:

On the question of balloting, there has been heavy criticism of the new 'triple lock' proposals (at least 50 per cent of constituency must have voted, a majority of those votes must be in favour, and, in 'essential services', at least 40 per cent of the constituency must have voted in favour). Contrast has been made with the democratic deficit of the general election. 331 of the 650 MPs were elected with less than an absolute majority, 50 were elected with less than 40 per cent of the votes cast for him or her, and one was elected with only 24.5 per cent of the votes cast in his favour…(Business Secretary) Sajid Javid failed to reach the proposed 40 per cent threshold, elected by just 38.3 per cent of his electorate. Half of the new Cabinet ministers would not have been elected to Parliament if the Tories' planned strike ballot rules had applied to the election.[226]

Chapter 24

Relax, don't do it!

Article 24

Everyone has the right to rest and leisure, including reasonable limitation of working hours and periodic holidays with pay.

According to research firm Mercer, Britons have the fewest public holidays in the world, except for Mexico.[227]

By 2011, Britons worked some of the longest full-time hours in Europe; but some of the shortest part-time. The Office for National Statistics points out that this is because of the 'growing prevalence of part-time work, as flexible hours have become more common', with the loss of more workers' rights as documented in Chapter 23. 'If you look at full-time work, it puts us the top of the biggest economies in (Europe)' for working hours (*Guardian*).[228]

A 2016 study by Glassdoor put Spain, Sweden, Austria, Finland and France at the top of the list for paid holiday entitlements. At the bottom were Switzerland, the UK, Netherlands, Portugal and Ireland. In 2017, the Trades Union Congress found that Britain comes 22nd out of 24 European countries for statutory maternal leave. In Belgium, Denmark, Estonia, France, Malta and Switzerland, mothers get three months paid leave. Czech, Hungarian and Polish mothers get four months. British mothers get six weeks; only Ireland and Slovakia give less pay to pregnant women.[229]

Unions fought to win entitlements for British workers over 18 years to 80 minutes uninterrupted rest during six-hour shifts. Thanks in part to Blairite work ethics, the research group Chiumento found that in 2008 only 16% of Britons were taking regular lunch breaks. The BBC article carrying the story cited others who reasoned that 'presenteeism' in a time of greater worker insecurity was partly to blame. Even though most bosses claim to be happy about workers taking breaks, most worked through lunch to get things done and look productive to their employer. In 2015, the private health provider BUPA published a survey of 2,000 full-time workers. It found that two-thirds regularly skip lunch. Even of those who do take a 20-minute or longer lunch break, 40% answer emails or make calls. By the afternoon, 30% of workers felt ill from skipping lunch; 40% reckoned it negatively affected productivity; and 52% said it put them in a bad mood.[230]

Britons are some of the least happy workers in Europe.

In 2005, Kelly Services concluded a 14,000-person survey of European workers. It found that Scandinavian and French workers are happiest, with Spanish, Dutch and Belgian employees being least happy. Britain came ahead of these but behind other countries in Europe. Researchers and engineers self-reported higher degrees of happiness (59% and 53%). Least happy were managers and customers services (45% and 38%). The main reason was pay: 36% said they were happy with their pay, 24% said they were happy with health benefits. Seven years later, ACAS (advice for employers and employees) reported that British workers are the least happy in Europe.[231]

CAN'T GET NO SATISFACTION

After the financial crisis, a 2012 survey across 20 European countries by NatCen Social Research put Britain 13th. Main reasons for job dissatisfaction were long-hours and low-to-zero pay for long-hours. Of the 48% who had put in overtime, 44% had not been paid. Since the crisis, work became more boring and less diverse according to a majority of British people. A significant number also said that work was invading their lives; they found it hard to 'switch off' and had taken a pay cut. Nearly 10 years earlier, Britons were putting in £23 billion in unpaid overtime each year, or £4500 per worker on average per year. By 2003, managers were losing nearly £8000, plant and machine operators £2200 and craftworkers £2800.[232]

Returning to job satisfaction, a study by the London School of Business (2015) finds that nearly 50% of Britons are unhappy at work and are looking for a career change. By far the biggest demographic is younger people, under 45. Sixty-eight per cent of 18-24 year-olds want to make a change, as do 65% of 25-34 year-olds and 52% of 35-44-year-olds. A 2016 study by the University of Sussex says 'that engaging in paid work comes at a significant psychological cost'. The authors note that 'work per se is negatively associated with ... well-being, such that we would rather be doing other things. That is to say, work really is disutility'.[233]

In 2017, ADP surveyed 9,900 Europeans across eight countries. Britain tied with France and Italy for being least satisfied. Dutch, Polish and Swiss workers were most satisfied. In the UK, the happiest professions are architecture/engineering, IT and telecoms, healthcare and manufacturing. The least satisfying are finance, retail/leisure/catering and education. Least satisfied workers are in the poorer areas: Northern Ireland (59% satisfied), Scotland (60%), the north east (61%) and Wales (66%).[234]

Chapter 25

Children: deepening the scar

Article 25

(1) Everyone has the right to a standard of living adequate for the health and well-being of himself and of his family, including food, clothing, housing and medical care and necessary social services, and the right to security in the event of unemployment, sickness, disability, widowhood, old age or other lack of livelihood in circumstances beyond his control.

(2) Motherhood and childhood are entitled to special care and assistance. All children, whether born in or out of wedlock, shall enjoy the same social protection.

This book has documented instances of state-deprivation against the health and wellbeing of individuals and families in terms of nutrition, housing, healthcare and social security. It has also documented how the top-down adherence to neoliberal economics and post-financial crisis austerity has created conditions in which once-prosperous individuals encounter deprivation. This chapter focuses on child wellbeing. Poverty was once described by then-chancellor Gordon Brown (New Labour) as a 'scar on the soul' of Britain. Brown's 'light-touch' financial regulation in part laid the basis for the financial crisis of 2008 and subsequent, needless austerity which hurt mothers and children.[235]

The US-based Institute of Health Metrics and Evaluation finds that British children are more likely to die before the age of five than in any other western European country, except Malta. Each year around 3,000 British children died before their first birthday. Stillbirth is another chronic problem, with Britain being the worst in Western Europe. Each year, 4,000 babies are stillborn. The charity MAMA Academy says that '1,000 babies could be saved per year if wards adopted their Growth Assessment Protocol', a programme to improve maternity care.[236]

With the headline, 'UK child health still amongst the worst in Europe', OnMedica cites a 2014 report by the Children and Young People's Health Forum. According to 2010 data, Britain's 'all-cause' mortality rate for 0-14-year-olds shifted from average 'to among the worst in Europe. The figures have since been updated but the situation is no better'. Quoting the report: 'If we compare ourselves with the country with the lowest mortality for children and young people, Sweden (after controlling for population size among other variables), we find that in the UK every day five children under the age of 14 die who would not die in Sweden'.[237]

The crises have their roots in economic policy. In 1999, the Institute for Fiscal Studies published a paper reviewing child poverty in the UK. The shattering conclusions coincide with what was then nearly three decades of economic deregulation, financialization and privatization. The study uses relative poverty as a measure and found that 'child poverty...has risen markedly in Britain in the last 30 years. By (1996), around one in three, or 4.3 million children, were living in poor households. This compares with child poverty rates of one in ten, corresponding to 1.4 million children, in 1968'. When using absolute poverty as a measure, it finds that despite macroeconomic growth, 'child poverty remains stagnant since the late 1970s'.[238]

The social consequences have been dire for the previous and present generations.

In 2000, the UN Children's Fund (UNICEF) ranked Britain 20th out of 23 so-called developed countries in its relative poverty index. The report was based on 1990s' data. It notes that in 20 years, poverty in Europe stabilized but in Britain it tripled. UNICEF researcher Anna Wright expressed 'surprise' at what she called 'the extraordinary variation between the top and the bottom'. In another report from 2000, UNICEF authors note that '(w)hile the UK is at the EU average on the benchmark of GDP per head, performance is worse than average for five of the seven child-specific indicators. On three, child poverty; worklessness and teenage birth rate, the UK's performance is in fact the worst in the EU'. The report notes that Britain 'stands out' on child poverty 'in that the increase in poverty was so large (over 40 per cent between 1986 and 1991) and...in that its starting level was already the highest in the EU'.[239]

The UN has six dimensions of child wellbeing: material, health and safety, educational, family and peer, behaviour risks and subjective wellbeing. In a 2007 study of 21 OECD countries, Britain ranked last: behind the US, Hungary, the Czech Republic and Greece. At the top were Netherlands, Sweden, Denmark and Finland. For material wellbeing, the UK ranked fourth-worst, above Poland, Hungary and Ireland (a country whose development Britain helped set back with centuries of brutal colonialism). At the top were Sweden, Norway, Finland and Denmark.[240]

Britain topped the list of countries whose children are at risk of 'obesity, substance abuse, violence, and sexual risk-taking'. The US, Belgium and Hungary followed. At least risk are Swedish, Polish and Dutch children. British children were at the bottom of the list for subjective wellbeing, behind Poland, France and the Czech Republic. Top of the list were the Netherlands, Spain and Greece. Specific to poorer households, Britain ranked second worst, next to the US; next came Italy, Ireland and Spain. At the top were Denmark, Finland, Norway and Sweden. On the issue of family relations, Britain was at the bottom, below the US, Czech Republic and Canada. The top countries were Italy, Portugal, Netherlands and Switzerland. Britain came next to highest (after the US) for the percentage of children living in single-parent households: Sweden and Denmark followed. Italy,

Greece and Spain had the lowest. Similar statistics applied for British children living in step-families. Britain also boasts the lowest percentage of children who find peers 'kind and helpful', followed by the Czech Republic, the US and France. At the top are Switzerland, Portugal and Austria.[241]

In 2014, UNICEF criticized the UK for its regression in child protection. Britain was ranked '25th out of 41 developed countries in its ability to protect young people from the effects of the recession', despite the fact that Britain has the fifth or sixth biggest economy in the world (depending on the year and measure). David Bull, director of UNICEF UK, said of the state of post-recession British children: 'It is no accident'.[242]

By 2015, 600,000 London children were malnourished and a further 3 million across the UK were at risk.[243]

Chapter 26

Indoctrination

Article 26

(1) Everyone has the right to education. Education shall be free, at least in the elementary and fundamental stages. Elementary education shall be compulsory. Technical and professional education shall be made generally available and higher education shall be equally accessible to all on the basis of merit.

(2) Education shall be directed to the full development of the human personality and to the strengthening of respect for human rights and fundamental freedoms. It shall promote understanding, tolerance and friendship among all nations, racial or religious groups, and shall further the activities of the United Nations for the maintenance of peace.

(3) Parents have a prior right to choose the kind of education that shall be given to their children.

British parents who refuse to force their children to endure overcrowded, underfunded, bullying, state-indoctrination prisons known as schools face stern punishments from the government, in violation of Article 26, subsection 3.[244]

In 2002, Tony Blair's government became the first to jail a mother (formerly sick with an addiction) over her alleged failure to get her children to attend school. By 2004, up to 10 parents, most of them (if not all) mothers, had been jailed.[245]

By 2009, after more than a decade of New Labour policies, eight out of 10 teenagers found school either boring, limiting or in need of change. The education authority Ofsted said that boredom and irrelevance could explain high levels of truancy.

According to a 2017 BBC study (that is, after nearly a decade of needless austerity), the number of classrooms in secondary schools hosting 36 pupils or more had trebled. Some schools host up to 46 pupils per class, adding stress and disruption to the mix.[246]

Fifty per cent of British children are bullied at school at some point by teachers or other children. One international survey (2015) found that 38% of British children had been physically abused by other children in a four-week period. The report concludes that British children are the least happy in school of the nations surveyed, even as compared with schools in Ethiopia and Algeria. Feelings of exclusion run high, with 49.9% feeling excluded within a four-week period. The closest competitor is Norway, at 33.5%. British children came last or close to last on a range of satisfaction criteria, including relations with teachers, self-esteem, appearance, relations with other children and subjects/quality of learning.[247]

Among the many stresses inflicted on children is standardized testing. More than half of 10 to 11 year-olds (2016 study) feel pressured to do well in tests. Nearly 60% cite nervousness, nearly 40% worry and 17% sadness/moodiness. Only 14% said they enjoyed tests.[248]

For these and other reasons, local authorities are reporting a 60+% increase in home-schooling in any given five-year period beginning 2002. The outgoing New Labour government tried to put a stop to parents taking action to protect their children's mental health, introducing what became the Children, Schools and Families Act 2010, which made it harder to home-school. By 2013, councils under the Tory government had taken 13,128 parents to court for failing to get their children into school during so-called term-time holidays; this is where parents are on leave from work and want to take their children on holiday with them but doing so clashes with school time.[249]

By 2015, the number had jumped to 16,430, of whom 76% were

found guilty; an increase of 22% from the previous year. The number of fines issued also rose by 30% between 2013 and 2014. The pro-indoctrination fanaticism of the government is such that a Department for Education spokesperson even claimed: '(missing) just one week a year from school can mean a child is a quarter less likely to achieve good GCSE grades, having a lasting effect on their life chances'. By 2015, the Tories had increased fines for parents who remove their children from school.[250]

Chapter 27

Cultural wealth

Article 27

(1) Everyone has the right freely to participate in the cultural life of the community, to enjoy the arts and to share in scientific advancement and its benefits.

(2) Everyone has the right to the protection of the moral and material interests resulting from any scientific, literary or artistic production of which he is the author.

A report from 2015 by Goldsmiths University and the foundation Create revealed that three-quarters of people working in the 'creative industries' come from wealthy backgrounds. Hadrian Garrad of Create also noted an alarming trend in the exploitation of poorer interns and apprentices in said industries: 'The scale of people who have worked for free or are working without a contract is pretty scary. And given how much more expensive it is to live in London, it is more and more likely that people without money will just not be able to follow careers in the arts'. Levels of ignorance are high. Just 12% of white participants in creative industries thought that ethnicity played a role in success, whereas 44% of black, Asian and ethnic minority (BAME) participants thought so.[251]

In terms of young people having access to arts and culture, social status again dominates. The UK's Social Mobility Commission (2016) found that 'while 84% of children from middle-class homes go to art galleries, the figure is 51% among poorer families' (BBC). In early-2017, Richard Russell of Arts Council England stated:[252]

Family background and level of education are both strong

indicators of whether children will go on to engage in arts and culture. Black and minority ethnic children are less likely than white children to be taken to an arts event by their parents when growing up. These are just two of the factors highlighted in our Equality and Diversity Report, as to why a number of our children miss out on engaging with arts and culture.[253]

As we have seen in previous chapters, ethnic minorities and people with so-called disabilities are likely to be poorer than their so-called able, ethnic majority counterparts.

Science is also the privilege of the rich. Once researchers land a paid position, they are paid on a fairly equal basis. However, entering the various science professions is less easy for people from poorer backgrounds. Forty-four per cent of UK Nobel Prize winners in the sciences were educated in fee-paying schools, despite those schools educating only 7% of the population. Katherine Mathieson of the British Science Association says that the 'class barrier' is 'more extreme for science' than for other professions. Most 10-14 year-olds find science interesting, but few from poor backgrounds entertain entering the profession. In 2012, university tuition fees tripled. 'I suspect that fees could be a massive deterrent to those who grow up in families that have to worry about the basic level of income', says Mathieson.[254]

Chapter 28

The social order

Article 28

Everyone is entitled to a social and international order in which the rights and freedoms set forth in this Declaration can be fully realized.

Article 28 cannot be realized in the UK because since the end of the Wilson government in the 1970s, the UK's political class, including unelected advisers, have formulated policies which put money and personal profit-making at the centre of virtually all laws and regulations. Exceptions, such as the NHS, occur only when sufficient opposition can be mustered from the grassroots.

These policies are the result of a deep-rooted ideology among Tories, Liberals and centrist Labourites. The Lib Dem Manifesto for the 2017 General Election, for instance, outlined their commitment to turning publicly-owned services over to private interests. The ideology is so deep-rooted that even though a majority of Britons want to own most services, the Lib Dems pledged to privatize new initiatives: 'Additional funding to bring more private investment into renewable energy. £5 billion of initial capital for a new British Housing and Infrastructure Development Bank, using public money to attract private investment for these priorities'. Former Lib Dem Business Secretary Sir Vince Cable is a former chief economist at Shell. He also wrote policy papers for the Royal Institute of International Affairs advocating a form of Anglo-American-led neoliberal globalization opposed to 'economic autarky', or independence. As further proof, a famous YouGov poll which shows that most Britons favour public ownership of energy, water, postal and health services, also shows that more Liberal

Democrat supporters than far-right UKIP supporters advocate privatization over public ownership.[255]

THE NEW CONSERVATISM

By far the wealthiest and most dangerous party is the Conservative party (Tories). For centuries, the wealthy establishment ruled over peasants with comparative ease. According to the National Archives, as late as the early-eighteenth century, 3% of Britons had the right to vote: the aristocracy. It would not be until 1884 with the passing of the Third Reform Act that working men over the age of 21 won the right to vote, following Chartism and related movements. The Labour Party emerged in this context. Historians ignore these minor details and persist the rumour that Britain is somehow the world's oldest democracy.[256]

By the 1980s, with the country locked into a 'free market' ideology, Tory policymakers were advocating a 'new Conservatism' in an effort to beat back Labourite socialism. Their speeches from the period provide a valuable insight into the ideologies driving Tory and so-called New Labour (or Blairite) politics. They make it clear that social rights and freedoms are not the purview of government, except freedoms for the wealthy and successful, and are therefore anathema to Article 28 of the UDHR.

Speaking to the right-wing think tank Bow Group in 1980, Treasury Secretary Nigel Lawson, explained: 'During the 25 years that followed Churchill', himself a right-wing, anti-socialist fanatic, 'the philosophy of social democracy' emerged from the grassroots. Social democracy was rooted 'in the efficacy of government action', meaning governments of left-leaning parties reflecting the wishes of working people, 'and its deep commitment to the notion of "equality"'. Notice Lawson's dismissive placing of the word equality into quote marks. For a while, the Tories 'embraced both these delusions', says Lawson. But there were reasons to be cheerful because 'the old consensus is in the process of being re-established', namely a 'return to the mainstream'; meaning back to the good old days of aristocratic control in which the masses serve elite interests. The so-called New Conservatism was, according to Lawson, 'founded on the basic acceptance of the ineradicable imperfection of human nature', meaning everyone for themselves. This includes 'scepticism about radical plans of any kind'. The ideology also opposes 'bring(ing) all social...relationships within the political realm'; hence Thatcher's no such thing as society speech not long after.[257]

The aftermath of the financial crisis of 2008 gave the Tories an excuse to transfer more public wealth to the private sector under the pretext of necessary austerity, many of the human costs have been documented in this book.

Chapter 29

No such thing as society

Article 29

(1) Everyone has duties to the community in which alone the free and full development of his personality is possible.

(2) In the exercise of his rights and freedoms, everyone shall be subject only to such limitations as are determined by law solely for the purpose of securing due recognition and respect for the rights and freedoms of others and of meeting the just requirements of morality, public order and the general welfare in a democratic society.

(3) These rights and freedoms may in no case be exercised contrary to the purposes and principles of the United Nations.

In the 1980s, the Conservatives formally abandoned any pretence of their duty to the community when leader and PM Margaret Thatcher (in)famously announced:

> too many children and people have been given to understand "I have a problem, it is the Government's job to cope with it!" or "I have a problem, I will go and get a grant to cope with it!" "I am homeless, the Government must house me!" and so they are casting their problems on society and who is society? There is no such thing! There are individual men and women and there are families and no government can do anything except through people and people look to themselves first. It is our duty to look after ourselves and then also to help look after our neighbour and life is a reciprocal business and people have got the entitlements too much in mind without the obligations.[258]

When Thatcher said 'too many children and people', she was referring to the working and middle classes. The upper classes believe in their own entitlements to inherited wealth, low taxes, state subsidies for their failing businesses and stock dividends accrued from privatized public services. Thatcher and her supporters believed and continue to believe that the law should work only in their favour; that government must exist in order to stop, say, homeless people from sleeping in Buckingham Palace; but at the same time government must not help people from becoming homeless. If they cannot be turned into profitable commodities (through social impact bonds or prison labour), the poor can be left to die as they are a drain on upper class profits.

Since the end of World War II, the Labour Party has been split between those who believe in the kind of democratic state-socialism that rebuilt Britain and made it a world leader in public health (the Bennites) and those who believe that Labour should be Tory-lite (call them the Healeyites).[d] With massive amounts of American money and ideological backing, the Healeyite faction of the Labour Party won and by the mid-1990s, the corporate class and mega-wealthy were relying on Tony Blair with his New Labour brand of neoliberalism to perpetuate their wealth under the banner of 'socialism'.

Blair revoked Clause IV, which hitherto committed the Labour Party (and thus any Labour government) to socialist principles, including state-ownership.

This book has documented the social costs.

Conclusion

Article 30

Nothing in this Declaration may be interpreted as implying for any State, group or person any right to engage in any activity or to perform any act aimed at the destruction of any of the rights and freedoms set forth herein.

Every year, Barclays publishes a wealth map of the UK. In 2016, it found that 690,000 Britons had made it to the millionaire class: that's about the number of British children experiencing malnutrition. The map includes areas in which rising house prices and wealth-generation are benefiting thousands of people. In response, Akshaya Bhargava, a chief executive at Barclays' Wealth, Entrepreneurs and Business Banking section, enthused: 'As we look at the future of global trade and inward investment it is the success of our entrepreneurs that will help drive future prosperity'. Bhargava concluded: 'it is essential that business leaders and policy makers continue to nurture these growth areas in order to ensure that these trends continue'.[259]

As the Barclays map was published, Britain's oldest children's charity, Bernardo's, reaffirmed that a quarter of British children (nearly 4 million) live in poverty: 1.7 million of whom live in 'severe' poverty. The report notes that infants in families earning below £10,000 a year are more than twice as likely to suffer 'chronic illness' as those living in households earning over £52,000. Infant mortality is 10% higher for the poor than for middle-class infants. The report precedes a study by the Royal College of Paediatrics and Child Health, which notes that appalling housing conditions (including damp, overcrowding and infestations) coupled with unaffordable prices for quality foods are 'seriously affecting these children's health'. Shortly before the reports were published, Oxfam described Britain as 'one of the most unequal nations in the developed world'.[260]

The Conservative government subsequently announced plans to cut free school meals, a move estimated by the Education Policy Institute to affect at least 600,000 children from deprived families.[261]

Despite propaganda supporting what we might call the Bhargava model, that growing prosperity will spread, the government's own Social Mobility Commission (2016) inadvertently agrees with Oxfam: that inequality is self-perpetuating. Not only is it self-perpetuating, it has become the dominant ideology of the British state, which is driven by deregulation and financial markets. 'It has long been assumed that Britain can get by with economic growth that is exclusive not inclusive', says the report. 'Over decades, a quiet new assumption has come to underpin public policy thinking: that people from weaker economic areas who wanted to (succeed) would have to move out'. The assessment is compounded by figures from 2011 to 2014, which show that 49,789 London-based families were forced to leave their homes due to both soaring rents and social security cuts. Leaked documents quoted in the *Independent* show that many are sent (sometimes hundreds of miles away) from their friends and family to start new lives in lower-cost areas. The paper notes that '(as) the figures refer to families, the number of children moved is likely to be in the hundreds of thousands'. Some have dubbed it 'social cleansing'.[262]

The Social Mobility Commission report concludes that '(a) less divided Britain will require a more redistributive approach to spreading education and employment prospects across our country'. Less than year later, the Conservative government announced plans to maintain Britain's deep-rooted class divide by promoting grammar schools, which are known to privilege the well-off. Publicly, the report's recommendations for a more equitable distribution of wealth are dismissed as hard-left extremism by corporate- and state-owned media. Politically, the only people advocating such a policy are those in the socialist faction of the Labour Party.[263]

The economic shocks caused by our highly volatile, deregulated economy are coupled with crushing austerity policies which enrich Britain's wealthiest (who lobby for such reforms) and steal from Britain's neediest (who are too poor and fragmented to fight back). As a result of a decade of post-financial crisis reforms, life expectancy has fallen for men and women over 65 years of age, according to the Office for National Statistics. While the cold usually kills 20,000 elderly people each winter in the UK, 2015-16 killed off 140,000. These figures followed a pledge by the Conservative government to eliminate the annual, meagre winter fuel allowance for millions of British pensioners.[264]

The drive towards social brutality has been slowed by the Tory government's own hubris. When middle-class and older people alike realized that Tory proposals would hurt them and their families out to 2022, they voted Labour in the general election of 2017. Labour was unusual in that a dedicated socialist, Jeremy Corbyn, had fought off successive coup attempts by centrists and right-wingers within the Parliamentary Labour Party, who were acting against the wishes of hundreds of thousands of grassroots Labour Party supporters.

Momentum, the grassroots youth-led organization, fought a social media campaign to get under-30s excited about politics for the first time in their lives. These factors combined to rob the Tory government of its majority in the general election of 2017, forcing it to bribe the obscure DUP party of Northern Ireland into a power-sharing deal.

Although Labour failed to win a majority or plurality (by less than 3% of the vote share in the case of the latter), it succeeded in forcing the Tories to rethink their cruel policies, such as imposing hunger on half a million more children and cutting winter fuels for pensioners. This shows that as long as people are apathetic and allow Blairite right-wingers like Ed Miliband (former Labour leader) to dominate, the country will continue on a path towards all-out privatization and eventual collapse. When people choose to pressure the least worst option (that is, the Labour Party) to humanize the political system, big changes can occur within rigid systems. A Labour victory, led by socialists and pressured to stay on course by a dedicated public, would be just the first step towards a better political system.

Endnotes

a   Unlawfully, because, as HRW notes, it violates the Human Rights Act 1998, which at the time of writing the Tory government is seeking to dismantle.

b   The latter supposedly fall short of complete reduction of liberties and do not therefore require the government to issue a state of emergency and thereby justify their issuance to the European Convention on Human Rights.

c   We know that in many cases they are. See, for instance, former Chatham House Fellow Mark Curtis's book, *Secret Affairs* (2010, Serpent's Tail).

d   After Tony Benn and Denis Healey, respectively.

1.   UN ICCPR 1966, https://treaties.un.org/pages/ViewDetails.aspx?src=IND&mtdsg_no=IV-4&chapter=4&lang=en. Roosevelt quoted in Mary Ann Glendon, 2001, *A World Made New*, Random House.

2.   UN, 'The Foundation of International Human Rights Law', http://www.un.org/en/sections/universal-declaration/foundation-international-human-rights-law/.

3.   Labour's Keir Starmer, for instance, referred to 'core British values' including internationalism, cooperation, solidarity, 'unflinching commitment(s) to protect the fundamentals that make us proud to live in this country - human rights, workplace rights, our environment and the rule of law'. Keir Starmer, 'Speech at Chatham House: 'What next for Britain?'', 27 March 2017, http://press.labour.org.uk/post/158884928409/keir-starmer-speech-at-chatham-house-what-next.

4.   When the UN Committee on the Rights of Persons with Disabilities sent an ambassador to the UK, she was insulted and dismissed by the government and media. Raquel Rolnik, who is Brazilian, was called a 'Brazil nut' by the *Daily Mail*, a member of the 'loony left' by MP Michael Ellis, an 'idiot(...)'

by MP Philip Davies, a 'loopy Brazilian leftie...masquerading as a serious UN official' by MP Stewart Jackson and a worshipper of 'Candomble (sic, Candomblé), a religion linked to slavery that worships African gods' (*Daily Mail*. The religion is linked to slavery in that Africans enslaved by the Portuguese continued their traditions in Brazil). Jack Doyle, 'Now UN sparks fury after launching human rights investigation into Britain's disability benefit reforms', *Daily Mail*, 27 August 2014 and James Chapman and Steve Doughty, 'Outrage as "loopy" UN inspector lectures Britain: She's from violent, slum-ridden Brazil, yet still attacks us on housing and human rights', *Daily Mail*, 11 September 2013.

5. Myres S. McDougal and Gerhard Bebr, 'Human Rights in the United Nations', *The American Journal of International Law*, 1964, 58: 603-41, http://digitalcommons.law.yale.edu/cgi/viewcontent.cgi?article=3570&context=fss_papers.

6. Herbert W. Briggs, 'Implementation of the Proposed International Covenant on Human Rights', *The American Journal of International Law*, April 1948, 42(2): 389-397.

7. Margaret E. Galey, 'The Universal Declaration of Human Rights: The Role of Congress', *Political Science and Politics*, September 1998, 31(3): 524-29.

8. Antoon de Baets, 'The Impact of the Universal Declaration of Human Rights on the Study of History', *History and Theory*, February 2009, 48(1): 20-43. David P. Forsythe, 'Human Rights Fifty Years after the Universal Declaration', *Political Science and Politics*, September 1998, 31(3): 505-51. Marjorie M. Whiteman, 'Mrs. Franklin D. Roosevelt and the Human Rights Commission', *The American Journal of International Law*, October 1968, 62(4): 918-92.

9. House of Lords, 'Human Rights and Civil Liberties in the United Kingdom 2 July 2015', Library Note, http://research-briefings.parliament.uk/ResearchBriefing/Summary/LLN-2015-0016.

10. National Archives, 'What is the Universal Declaration?', http://webarchive.nationalarchives.gov.uk/20081223042927/http://equalityhumanrights.com/en/projects/universaldeclarationis60/Pages/WhatistheUNdeclaration.aspx.

11. Dominic Raab, 2008, *The Assault on Liberty: What Went Wrong with Rights*, 4th Estate, p. xviii.

12. National Archives, in the work cited.

13. In the same place.

14. In the same place.

15. Quoted in Gerald R. Taylor, 1997, *Labour's Renewal?: The Policy Review and Beyond*, Macmillan, pp. 170-3.

16. UN OHCHR, International Covenant on Civil and Political Rights, 2200A (XXI) 16 December 1966, http://www.ohchr.org/EN/ProfessionalInterest/Pages/CCPR.aspx and for reservations, UN Treaty Collection, Chapter IV Human Rights, ICCPR, https://treaties.un.org/pages/ViewDetails.aspx?src=IND&mtdsg_no=IV-4&chapter=4&lang=en#6.

17. In the same place.

18. Oliver Hawkins, 'Migration Statistics', House of Commons Library, Briefing Paper, No. SN06077, 29 June 2017. *Observer*, 'Benefits in Britain', 6 April 2013, https://www.theguardian.com/politics/2013/apr/06/welfare-britain-facts-myths. JRF, 'Housing Benefit claimants in work' in *Monitoring Poverty and Social Exclusion*, 23 November 2015, http://www.jrf.org.uk/data/housing-benefit-claimants-work.

19. BBC, 'Reality Check: Is UK still the world's fifth biggest economy?', 28 October 2016, http://www.bbc.co.uk/news/business-37763913. Theresa May, 'May v Corbyn: The Battle For Number 10 - The full programme', Sky News, 30 May 2017, https://www.youtube.com/watch?v=1mN_zZqlQts. Peter Walker, 'Dominic Raab accused of 'stupid and offensive' food bank comments', *Guardian*, 29 May 2017, https://www.theguardian.com/politics/2017/may/29/tory-mp-dominic-raab-jeered-over-food-bank-comments. JRF, '1.25 million peo-

ple are destitute in the UK', 27 April 2016, https://www.jrf.org.uk/press/destitute-uk.

20. Angela Monaghan and Jessica Elgot, "Brexit boom' gives Britain record 134 billionaires, fuelling inequality fears', *Guardian*, 7 May 2017, https://www.theguardian.com/business/2017/may/07/brexit-boom-creates-record-number-of-uk-billionaires-sunday-times-rich-list. ONS, 2015, *Compendium*, 'Chapter 2: Total wealth, Wealth in Great Britain, 2012 to 2014', https://www.ons.gov.uk/peoplepopulationandcommunity/personalandhouseholdfinances/incomeandwealth/compendium/wealthingreatbritainwave4/2012to2014/chapter2totalwealthwealthingreatbritain2012to2014. Nicholas Watt and Jill Treanor, 'Revealed: 50% of Tory funds come from City', *Guardian*, 8 February 2011, https://www.theguardian.com/politics/2011/feb/08/tory-funds-half-city-banks-financial-sector. Holly Watt, 'Conservatives' donors give 10 times as much as Labour's in one week', *Guardian*, 1 June 2017, https://www.theguardian.com/politics/2017/jun/01/conservatives-donors-give-10-times-as-much-as-labours-in-one-week.

21. UNESC, Committee on Economic, Social and Cultural Rights, 'Public debt, austerity measures and the International Covenant on Economic, Social and Cultural Rights', E/C.12/2016/1, 22 July 2016, https://documents-dds-ny.un.org/doc/UNDOC/GEN/G16/163/81/PDF/G1616381.pdf?OpenElement.

22. A.H. Halsey, 1986 (3rd), *Change in British Society*, Oxford University Press, pp. 31-45.

23. In the same place.

24. Eurostat, 'File: Life expectancy at birth, 1980–2014 (years) YB16.png', http://ec.europa.eu/eurostat/statistics-explained/index.php/File:Life_expectancy_at_birth,_1980%E2%80%932014_(years)_YB16.png.

25. Eurostat, 'Infant mortality rates', 27 March 2017, http://appsso.eurostat.ec.europa.eu/nui/submitViewTa bleAction.do.

26. See my *Britain's Secret Wars*, 2016, Clairview Books.

27. KidsRights Index 2017, http://kidsrightsindex.org/
Portals/5/The%20KidsRights%20Index%202017.pd-
f?ver=2017-05-11-124125-077.

28. Dominic Richardson, Zlata Brukauf, Emilia Toczydlowska
and Yekaterina Chzhen, 'Comparing Child-focused Sustain-
able Development Goals (SDGs) in High-income Countries:
Indicator Development and Overview', Office of Research
Innocenti Working Paper WP-2017-08, June 2017, https://
www.unicef-irc.org/publications/pdf/IWP_2017-08.pdf. ONS,
'Live births women aged 'Under 18' and 'Under 20', (per
1,000 women aged 15 to 17 and 15 to 19) in EU28 countries,
2004, 2013 and 2014', 11 March 2016, https://www.ons.gov.
uk/peoplepopulationandcommunity/birthsdeathsandmar-
riages/livebirths/s/005466livebirthswomenagedunder18and-
under20per1000womenaged15to17and15to19ineu28countrie-
s200142013and2014

29. In the same place and UN Development Programme, 'Table 1:
Human Development Index and its components', http://hdr.
undp.org/en/composite/HDI.

30. The Commonwealth, 'United Kingdom: Constitution and politics', http://thecommonwealth.org/our-member-countries/
united-kingdom/constitution-politics. HMG, British Nationality Act 1948, www.legislation.gov.uk/ukpga/1948/56%2520/
pdfs/ukpga_19480056_en.pdf.

31. HMG, 'Crown Prerogative', http://www.parliament.uk/
site-information/glossary/crown-prerogative/.

32. HMG, 'Types of British nationality', https://www.gov.uk/
types-of-british-nationality/british-overseas-territories-citi-
zen.

33. House of Lords, Judgments - R (On The Application of Bancoult) V Secretary of State For Foreign and Commonwealth
Affairs, Session 2007-08, UKHL 61, https://www.publications.
parliament.uk/pa/ld200708/ldjudgmt/jd081022/banc-1.htm.

34. Stephen Allen, 2014, *The Chagos Islanders and International Law*, Bloomsbury. David Vine, 2009, *Island of Shame: The Secret History of the U.S. Military Base on Diego Garcia*, Princeton University Press.

35. Lords, in the work cited.

36. Maureen Tong, 'Self-determination in the post-colonial era: Prospects for Chagossians' in Sandra J.T.M. Evers and Mary Kooy (eds.), 2011, *Eviction from the Chagos Islands: Displacement and Struggle for Identity Against Two World Powers*, Brill, p. 165.

37. Vine, in the work cited.

38. Peter H. Sand, 2009, *United States and Britain in Diego Garcia: The Future of a Controversial Base*, Palgrave Macmillan, pp. 16-17.

39. John Pilger, 2006, *Freedom Next Time*, Black Swan, p. 62.

40. In the same place.

41. In the same place, p. 60.

42. Vine, in the work cited.

43. Lords, in the work cited, col. 163, https://www.publications.parliament.uk/pa/ld200708/ldjudgmt/jd081022/banc-7.htm.

44. Laurie Fransman QC, 2011 (3rd), *Fransman's British Nationality Law*, Bloomsbury Professional, p. 873 n10.

45. Ian Hendry and Susan Dickson, 2011, *British Overseas Territories Law*, Hart Publishing, p. 19.

46. WikiLeaks, 'HMG floats proposal for marine reserve covering the Chagos Archipelago', 15 May 2009, https://wikileaks.org/plusd/cables/09LONDON1156_a.html.

47. Hajira Amla, 'Chagossians on shaky ground after Mauritius-UK tribunal ruling, says Seychelles association', 26 March 2015, http://www.seychellesnewsagency.com/articles/2629/Chagossians+on+shaky+ground+after+Mauritius-UK+tribunal+ruling,+says+Seychelles+association.

48. BBC, 'Half of young black people unemployed, says report', 20 January 2010, http://news.bbc.co.uk/1/hi/uk/8468308.stm. BBC, 'Row over UK 'racism'', 23 August 2000, http://news.bbc.

co.uk/1/hi/uk_politics/891943.stm.

49. Matthew Taylor, '50% rise in long-term unemployment for young ethnic minority people in UK', *Guardian*, 10 March 2015, https://www.theguardian.com/society/2015/mar/10/50-rise-in-long-term-unemployed-youngsters-from-uk-ethnic-minorities.

50. Ami Sedghi, 'Ethnic minorities face barriers to social mobility and job opportunities', *Guardian*, 12 June 2014, https://www.theguardian.com/education/2014/jun/12/ethnic-minorities-social-mobility-employment. Stephen J. Hunt, 2017 (2nd), *The Life Course: A Sociological Introduction*, Palgrave Macmillan, p. 191.

51. Committee on the Elimination of Racial Discrimination, 'Concluding observations on the twenty-first to twenty-third periodic reports of United Kingdom', CERD/C/GBR/CO/21-23, August 2016, https://www.equalityhumanrights.com/sites/default/files/icerd-_concluding_observations.pdf.

52. Dame Louise Casey, 'The Casey Review: A review into opportunity and integration', December 2016, p. 148, https://www.gov.uk/government/uploads/system/uploads/attachment_data/file/575973/The_Casey_Review_Report.pdf.

53. Robert Verkaik, 'UN says sexual discrimination is rife in Britain', *Independent*, 1 September 2008, www.independent.co.uk/news/uk/home-news/un-says-sexual-discrimination-is-rife-in-britain-915800.html.

54. Katie Allen, 'Equal pay for women not likely till 2067, says research', *Guardian*, 19 August 2010, https://www.theguardian.com/uk/2010/aug/19/equal-pay-women-2057.

55. Emily Dugan, 'More than half of women are discriminated against at work', *Independent*, 29 December 2013, www.independent.co.uk/news/uk/home-news/more-than-half-of-women-are-discriminated-against-at-work-9029535.html. Tracy McVeigh and Toby Helm, 'Recession hits middle-aged women worst, new research finds', *Guardian*, 8 July 2012,

https://www.theguardian.com/society/2012/jul/08/reces-sion-hits-middle-aged-women-hardest.

56. BBC, 'UN Special Rapporteur Rashida Manjoo says UK has 'sexist culture'', 15 April 2014, http://www.bbc.co.uk/news/uk-27034117.

57. OECD, 'Government at a Glance 2015', 6 July 2015, http://www.oecd-ilibrary.org/governance/government-at-a-glance-2015/women-in-politics_gov_glance-2015-24-en.

58. Asa Bennett, 'United Nations Probing UK Over 'Grave' Human Rights Violations Of Disabled', *Huffington Post*, 28 August 2014, www.huffingtonpost.co.uk/2014/08/28/un-dwp-benefits-disabled-human-rights-probe_n_5727580.html. For Rolnik, see note 4 above.

59. JRF, 'Monitoring poverty and social exclusion in the UK 2005', 13 December 2005, https://www.jrf.org.uk/report/monitor-ing-poverty-and-social-exclusion-uk-2005.

60. EHRC, 2010, *How Fair is Britain?*, 'Chapter 10', https://www.equalityhumanrights.com/sites/default/files/how_fair_is_britain_-_complete_report.pdf.

61. Leigh Day and Co., 'The Purple Workforce', October 2014, https://www.leighday.co.uk/LeighDay/media/LeighDay/doc-uments/Disability/Disability-report_v9_FINAL_rev_online.pdf.

62. BBC, 'Lord Freud: Disabled people 'not worth full wage'', 15 October 2014, http://www.bbc.co.uk/news/av/uk-poli-tics-29631573/lord-freud-disabled-people-not-worth-full-wage.

63. BBC, 'No final Grenfell Tower death toll this year, police say', 28 June 2017, http://www.bbc.co.uk/news/uk-40434741.

64. Michelle Roberts, 'UK air pollution 'linked to 40,000 early deaths a year'', BBC, 23 February 2016, http://www.bbc.co.uk/news/health-35629034.

65. Ministry of Defence, 'Strategic Trends Programme: 2007 to 2036', January 2007, www.cuttingthroughthematrix.com/arti-

cles/strat_trends_23jan07.pdf.

66. BBC, 'Liverpool Care Pathway: "They told my family I was dying"', 15 August 2013, http://www.bbc.co.uk/news/health-23698071.

67. Anuji Varma, 'Rustie Lee accuses Birmingham doctors of wrongly trying to let her mum die', *Birmingham Mail*, 31 October 2012, http://www.birminghammail.co.uk/news/local-news/rustie-lees-mum-was-wrongly-put-276419.

68. Steve Doughty, 'Top doctor's chilling claim: The NHS kills off 130,000 elderly patients every year', *Daily Mail*, 20 June 2012, http://www.dailymail.co.uk/news/article-2161869/Top-doctors-chilling-claim-The-NHS-kills-130-000-elderly-patients-year.html.

69. Leon Watson, 'Pensioner placed on Liverpool Care Pathway WITHOUT family's permission dies after spending eight days without food or water', *Daily Mail*, 6 March 2013, http://www.dailymail.co.uk/news/article-2289033/Pensioner-placed-Liverpool-Care-Pathway-WITHOUT-familys-permission-dies-spending-days-food-water.html.

70. Peter Stanford, 'Families left grieving and angry by the Liverpool Care Pathway', *Telegraph*, 29 October 2012, http://www.telegraph.co.uk/news/health/9635842/Families-left-grieving-and-angry-by-the-Liverpool-Care-Pathway.html.

71. Office for National Statistics, 'Excess Winter Mortality in England and Wales: 2012-13 (Provisional) and 2011-12 (Final)', 26 November 2013, https://www.ons.gov.uk/peoplepopulationandcommunity/birthsdeathsandmarriages/deaths/bulletins/excesswintermortalityinenglandandwales/2013-11-26. Fraser Nelson, 'Dying of the cold: a very British disease', *Spectator*, 30 March 2013, https://blogs.spectator.co.uk/2013/03/dying-of-the-cold-a-very-british-disease/. J.D. Healy, 'Excess winter mortality in Europe: a cross country analysis identifying key risk factors', *Journal of Epidemiology and Community Health* (BMJ Group), 2003, Vol. 57, pp.784-9.

72. Emily Gosden, 'Green Deal energy efficiency scheme a "disappointing failure"', *Telegraph*, 15 September 2014, http://www.telegraph.co.uk/news/earth/energy/11095359/Green-Deal-energy-efficiency-scheme-a-disappointing-failure.html. Huhne quoted in Peter Hall, 2014, *Good Cities, Better Lives: How Europe Discovered the Lost Art of Urbanism*, Routledge, p. 35.

73. CORE, 'Modern slavery in supply chains', no date, http://corporate-responsibility.org/issues/modern-slavery-bill/.

74. Global Slavery Index 2014, https://www.globalslaveryindex.org.

75. Justin Rowlatt and Jane Deith, 'The bitter story behind the UK's national drink', BBC News, 8 September 2015, http://www.bbc.co.uk/news/world-asia-india-34173532. Jane Deith, 'UK tea brands drop Indian supplier over work conditions', BBC, 14 January 2016, http://www.bbc.co.uk/news/business-35235293. Justin Rowlatt, 'Indian tea workers' conditions remain very poor', BBC, 12 November 2016, http://www.bbc.co.uk/news/world-asia-india-37936349.

76. Pete Pattisson, 'Aid money for development projects in Nepal linked to child labour', *Guardian*, 12 February 2015, https://www.theguardian.com/global-development/2015/feb/12/aid-money-development-projects-nepal-child-labour. ITV, 'Abuse uncovered at Bangladesh factory with links to UK brand', 6 February 2014, http://www.itv.com/news/story/2014-02-06/exposure-bangladesh-factory-abuse/.

77. Campaign Against Prison Slavery, http://www.webarchive.org.uk/ukwa/target/61833275/source/subject.

78. In the same place.

79. In the same place and Grahame Allen and Chris Watson, 'UK prison population statistics', Briefing Paper, No. SN/SG/04334, 20 April 2017, https://researchbriefings.files.parliament.uk/documents/SN04334/SN04334.pdf.

80. On Kenya, see this memo from the period: 'Emergency - Decypher (sic) of Telegram to the Secretary of State', 17 Jan-

uary 1955, http://www.scribd.com/doc/52818586/eight-of-fices-implicated-in-murder-and-abuse-in-Kenya?in_collection=2964763. On Northern Ireland, see Ian Cobain, 2012, *Cruel Britannia*, Portobello. On the torture of foreigners, see my *Britain's Secret Wars*, 2016, Clairview. On Diego Garcia, see Peter H. Sand, 'Diego Garcia: British–American Legal Black Hole in the Indian Ocean?', *Journal of Environmental Law*, 2009, 21(1): 113-37.

81. Sand, in the work cited.

82. Martin Scheinin, 'Promotion and protection of all human rights...', OHCHR, A/HRC/10/3, 4 February 2009, http://www2.ohchr.org/english/issues/terrorism/rapporteur/docs/A.HRC.10.3.pdf.

83. UNCTAD, 'Concluding observations on the fifth periodic report of the United Kingdom...', 24 June 2013, CAT/C/GBR/CO/5, www2.ohchr.org/english/bodies/cat/docs/co/CAT.C.GBR.CO.R.5-%20AUV_en.doc.

84. UNCTAD, 'Committee against torture concludes thirty-ninth session', 23 November 2007, http://www.unog.ch/unog/website/news_media_archive.nsf/%28httpNewsByYear_en%29/C125763C00590FD6C125739C0054A81C?OpenDocument.

85. Matthew Weaver, 'Timeline of Taser controversies in the UK', *Guardian*, 16 August 2016, https://www.theguardian.com/world/2016/aug/16/timeline-of-taser-controversies-in-the-uk. Independent Police Complaints Commission, 'IPCC review of Taser complaints and incidents: 2004-2013', https://www.ipcc.gov.uk/sites/default/files/Documents/guidelines_reports/Taser_report_final_2014.pdf.

86. Jon Robins, 'Majority of suspects Tasered by police are mentally ill, figures show', *Independent*, 26 December 2015, http://www.independent.co.uk/news/uk/crime/majority-of-suspects-tasered-by-police-are-mentally-ill-figures-show-a6786996.html.#

87. Peter Yeung, 'UK police used tasers on hundreds of minors

over past two years', *Independent*, 24 April 2016, http://www.
independent.co.uk/news/uk/home-news/police-tasers-mi-
nors-children-a6999061.html.

88. *Guardian* report from the period, quoted in Giulia Lotti, 'Tough
on young offenders: harmful or helpful?', Warwick Economic Research Papers, No. 1126, July 2016, https://www2.war-
wick.ac.uk/fac/soc/economics/research/workingpapers/2016/
twerp_1126_lotti.pdf.

89. Children's Commissioner, 'Placing young offenders in isolation hinders rehabilitation', 22 October 2015, https://www.
childrenscommissioner.gov.uk/2015/10/22/placing-young-of-
fenders-in-isolation-hinders-rehabilitation/.

90. UN Committee on Economic, Social and Cultural Rights,
'Concluding observations on the sixth periodic report of the
United Kingdom of Great Britain and Northern Ireland', 14
July 2016, E/C.12/GBR/CO/6,

91. Barry Reay, 1998, *Popular Cultures in England, 1550-1750*,
Routledge, p. 188. Owen Bowcott, 'Magistrates resign over
court charges that encourage innocent to plead guilty', *Guardian*, 31 July 2015, https://www.theguardian.com/law/2015/
jul/31/magistrates-resign-court-charges-encourage-inno-
cent-plead-guilty.

92. Law Society, 'High Court: government's residence test for
legal aid unlawful', 14 July 2014, http://www.lawsociety.org.
uk/news/stories/high-court-government-s-residence-test-for-
legal-aid-unlawful/.

93. Monidipa Fouzder, 'Court of Appeal dismisses criminal legal aid challenge', *Law Society Gazette*, 25 March 2015, https://
www.lawgazette.co.uk/law/court-of-appeal-dismisses-crimi-
nal-legal-aid-challenge/5047841.article.

94. Owen Bowcott, 'MoJ plan for legal aid residence test thrown
out by supreme court', *Guardian*, 18 April 2016, https://www.
theguardian.com/law/2016/apr/18/uk-supreme-court-throws-
out-legal-aid-residence-test-justice-minister-michael-gove.

95. UN Equality and Human Rights Commission, 'Socio-economic rights in the UK', April 2016, http://tbinternet.ohchr.org/Treaties/CESCR/Shared%20Documents/GBR/INT_CESCR_IFN_GBR_23989_E.pdf.

96. Howard League, 'Do better, do less', 2009, http://howardleague.org/wp-content/uploads/2016/04/Do-Better-Do-Less-low-res.pdf.

97. Social Exclusion Unit, 'Reducing re-offending by ex-prisoners', 2002, Office of the Deputy Prime Minister, http://www.bristol.ac.uk/poverty/downloads/keyofficialdocuments/Reducing%20Reoffending.pdf.

98. Alan Travis, 'Prison population surge raises threat of budget cuts', *Guardian*, 27 January 2012, https://www.theguardian.com/society/2012/jan/27/rise-prisoners-budget-cuts. Randeep Ramesh, 'More black people jailed in England and Wales proportionally than in US', *Guardian*, 11 October 2010, https://www.theguardian.com/society/2010/oct/11/black-prison-population-increase-england.

99. Inquest, 'BAME deaths in police custody', live document, http://www.inquest.org.uk/statistics/bame-deaths-in-police-custody. IRR, 'Criminal Justice System Statistics', http://www.irr.org.uk/research/statistics/criminal-justice/.

100. David Batty, 'Muslims report discrimination in prisons as fear of 'extremism' grows', *Guardian*, 6 July 2016, https://www.theguardian.com/society/2016/jul/06/muslims-discrimination-uk-prisons-extremism. HRW, 'Without suspicion', 4 July 2010, https://www.hrw.org/report/2010/07/04/without-suspicion/stop-and-search-under-terrorism-act-2000.

101. Jon Swaine, 'Women are under-paid and under-represented in Britain, says UN report', *Telegraph*, 2 September 2008, http://www.telegraph.co.uk/news/uknews/2666329/Women-are-under-paid-and-under-represented-in-Britain-says-UN-report.html.

102. BBC, 'UN Special Rapporteur Rashida Manjoo says UK has

'sexist culture', 15 April 2014, http://www.bbc.co.uk/news/uk-27034117.

103. Committee on the Rights of Persons with Disabilities, 'Inquiry concerning the United Kingdom of Great Britain and Northern Ireland carried out by the Committee under article 6 of the Optional Protocol to the Convention', 6 October 2016, CRPD/C/17/R.3, http://tbinternet.ohchr.org/_layouts/treatybodyexternal/Download.aspx?symbolno=CRPD%2f-C%2f17%2fR.3&Lang=en.

104. Brian Milligan, 'Benefit sanctions force people to sleep rough, claims charity', BBC, 11 December 2015, http://www.bbc.co.uk/news/business-35063040.

105. John Woodhouse and Noel Dempsey, 'Domestic violence in England and Wales', House of Commons Library, Briefing Paper, No. 6337, 6 May 2016.

106. Frances Ryan, 'They've endured domestic violence. Now they're victims of austerity', Guardian, 26 January 2017, https://www.theguardian.com/commentisfree/2017/jan/26/endured-domestic-violence-victims-austerity-sunderland

107. Woodhouse and Dempsey, in the work cited.

108. Rights of Women, 'Court deals blow to rights of domestic violence survivors to access justice', http://rightsofwomen.org.uk/court-deals-blow-rights-domestic-violence-survivors-access-justice/.

109. Liberty, 'Extended pre-charge detention', https://www.liberty-human-rights.org.uk/human-rights/countering-terrorism/extended-pre-charge-detention. HMG, 'Being arrested: your rights', https://www.gov.uk/arrested-your-rights/how-long-you-can-be-held-in-custody.

110. In the same place.

111. Rebecca Ratcliffe, 'Babar Ahmad returns to UK after being sentenced for supporting terror groups', Guardian, 19 July 2015, https://www.theguardian.com/uk-news/2015/jul/19/babar-ahmad-returns-after-jail-sentence-in-us-for-sup-

porting-terrorist-groups.

112. Robert Verkaik, 'The trials of Babar Ahmad', *Guardian*, 19 March 2016, https://www.theguardian.com/uk-news/2016/mar/12/babar-ahmad-jihad-bosnia-us-police-interview.

113. Working Group on Arbitrary Detention, 'The Working Group on Arbitrary Detention Deems the deprivation of liberty of Mr. Julian Assange as arbitrary', UN OHCHR, 5 February 2016, http://www.ohchr.org/EN/NewsEvents/Pages/DisplayNews.aspx?NewsID=17012&LangID=E.

114. Esther Addley, Jessica Elgot and Owen Bowcott, 'Julian Assange accuses UK minister of insulting UN after detention finding', *Guardian*, 5 February 2016, https://www.theguardian.com/media/2016/feb/05/julian-assange-accuses-philip-hammond-insulting-united-nations.

115. Justice, 'Secret Evidence', June 2009, https://2bquk8c-dew6192tsu41lay8t-wpengine.netdna-ssl.com/wp-content/uploads/2015/07/Secret-Evidence-10-June-2009.pdf

116. In the same place.

117. Dominic Casciani, 'Secret trial: One off – or the first of many?', BBC Online, 10 February 2016, http://www.bbc.co.uk/news/uk-35536278.

118. Directorate-general for Internal Policies, 'National security and secret evidence in legislation and before the courts: exploring the challenges', LIBE Committee, European Parliament, 2014, http://www.europarl.europa.eu/RegData/etudes/STUD/2014/509991/IPOL_STU%282014%29509991_EN.pdf.

119. Owen Bowcott, 'Rendition: government evidence to be heard in secret in UK for first time', *Guardian*, 23 March 2017, https://www.theguardian.com/world/2017/mar/23/rendition-government-evidence-heard-secret-uk-first-time. Owen Bowcott, 'What are secret courts and what do they mean for UK justice?', *Guardian*, 14 June 2013, https://www.theguardian.com/law/2013/jun/14/what-are-secret-courts.

120. See my *Britain's Secret Wars*, 2016, Clairview Books.

121. Philip Alston, 'Addendum: Study on targeted killings', Report of the Special Rapporteur on extrajudicial, summary or arbitrary executions, 28 May 2010, Human Rights Council, Fourteenth Session, United Nations General Assembly, A/HRC/14/24/Add.6, http://www2.ohchr.org/english/bodies/hrcouncil/docs/14session/A.HRC.14.24.Add6.pdf.

122. *Britain's Secret Wars*, in the work cited.

123. In the same place.

124. In the same place.

125. In the same place.

126. In the same place.

127. Alice Ross, 'MPs call on Theresa May to release 'kill list' for UK drone strikes', *Guardian*, 23 February 2017, https://www.theguardian.com/world/2017/feb/23/mps-theresa-may-release-kill-list-for-uk-drone-strikes.

128. Larisa Brown, 'Secret RAF drone strikes take out British jihadis', *Daily Mail*, 23 February 2017, http://www.dailymail.co.uk/news/article-4251122/Our-pilots-working-way-kill-list-UK-jihadis.html.

129. Duncan Campbell and Patrick Forbes, 'New Whitehall Bunker', *New Statesman*, 1985, http://www.duncancampbell.org/menu/journalism/newstatesman/newstatesman-1985/mail%20order%20war.pdf.

130. On the Five Eyes, see Loring Wirbel, 2001, *Star Wars*, Pluto Press. On Microsoft, Bill Blum, 2005, *Rogue State*, Zed Books.

131. Spencer Ackerman and James Ball, 'Optic Nerve: millions of Yahoo webcam images intercepted by GCHQ', *Guardian*, 28 February 2014, https://www.theguardian.com/world/2014/feb/27/gchq-nsa-webcam-images-internet-yahoo. Cara McGoogan, 'Why your smart TV is the perfect way to spy on you', *Telegraph*, 8 March 2017, http://www.telegraph.co.uk/technology/2017/03/08/smart-tv-perfect-way-spy/.

132. Marcel Rosenbach, Laura Poitras and Holger Stark, 'How the NSA Accesses Smartphone Data', *Der Spiegel*, 9 Sep-

tember 2013, http://www.spiegel.de/international/world/
how-the-nsa-spies-on-smartphones-including-the-black-
berry-a-921161.html.

133. Human Rights Council, 'The right to privacy in the digital
age', Report of the Office of the United Nations High Commissioner for Human Rights, 30 June 2014, A/HRC/27/37,
http://www.ohchr.org/EN/HRBodies/HRC/RegularSessions/
Session27/Documents/A.HRC.27.37_en.pdf.

134. Alan Travis, 'UN commissioner criticises decision to fast-track
emergency surveillance bill', *Guardian*, 16 July 2014, http://
www.theguardian.com/uk-news/2014/jul/16/un-commission-
er-criticises-decision-fast-track-emergency-surveillance-bill.

135. Adam Alexander, 'Digital surveillance "worse than Orwell"',
says new UN privacy chief', *Guardian*, 24 August 2015, https://
www.theguardian.com/world/2015/aug/24/we-need-geneva-
convention-for-the-internet-says-new-un-privacy-chief. UN
News Centre, 'Draft UK surveillance law threatens freedom of
expression, UN human rights experts warn', 12 January 2016,
http://www.un.org/apps/news/story.asp?NewsID=52982#.
WRI_eGkrLIU.

136. UN OHCHR, 'Report of the Special Rapporteur on the right
to privacy, Joseph A. Cannataci', Human Rights Council,
8 March 2016, www.ohchr.org/Documents/Issues/Priva-
cy/A-HRC-31-64.doc.

137. Amnesty International, 'United Kingdom: Submission for
the Review of Counter-terrorism and Security Powers', EUR
45/015/2010, 2010, https://www.amnesty.org.uk/files/septem-
ber_2010_-_review_of_counter_terrorism_and_security_pow-
ers.pdf.

138. Alexander Horne and Gavin Berman, 'Control orders and the
Prevention of Terrorism Act 2005', House of Commons Library, SN/HA/3438, 19 December 2011.

139. Nigel Morris, 'A control order ruined my life - and my respect
for Britain', *Independent*, 7 January 2011, http://www.indepen-

dent.co.uk/news/uk/home-news/a-control-order-ruined-my-life-ndash-and-my-respect-for-britain-2178069.html.

140. House of Lords and House of Commons Joint Committee on Human Rights, 'Post-Legislative Scrutiny: Terrorism Prevention and Investigation Measures Act 2011', Tenth Report of Session 2013-14, HL Paper 113, HC 1014, 23 January 2014, https://www.publications.parliament.uk/pa/jt201314/jtselect/jtrights/113/113.pdf.

141. Amnesty International, 'UK: TPIMs anti-terrorism plans would "seriously undermine" human rights', 4 September 2011, Press Release, https://www.amnesty.org.uk/press-releases/uk-tpims-anti-terrorism-plans-would-seriously-undermine-human-rights.

142. Ruud Lubbers, 'Asylum and elections', UNHRC, 2 July 2001, http://www.unhcr.org/uk/news/editorial/2001/7/3b4c06a919/asylum-elections.html.

143. Rowena Mason, 'Asylum UK immigration bill could create 'climate of ethnic profiling' – UNHCR', *Guardian*, 26 December 2013, https://www.theguardian.com/uk-news/2013/dec/26/uk-immigration-bill-climate-ethnic-profiling-unhcr.

144. Sam Jones, 'UN human rights chief denounces Sun over Katie Hopkins "cockroach" column', *Guardian*, 24 April 2015, https://www.theguardian.com/global-development/2015/apr/24/katie-hopkins-cockroach-migrants-denounced-united-nations-human-rights-commissioner.

145. Oliver Hawkins, 'Asylum Statistics', House of Common Library, Briefing Paper, No. SN01403, 30 March 2017.

146. Refugee Council, 'Tell it like it is: The truth about asylum', June 2015, https://www.refugeecouncil.org.uk/assets/0003/4969/Ref_C_TILII_June_2015.pdf.

147. Catrin Nye, 'The secret world of the UK's immigration removal centres', BBC Online, 12 May 2014, http://www.bbc.co.uk/news/uk-27332370.

148. Stephanie J. Silverman, 'Immigration detention in the UK',

Briefing Paper, Migration Observatory, Oxford University, 2 May 2017, http://www.migrationobservatory.ox.ac.uk/wp-content/uploads/2016/04/Briefing-Immigration_Detention-2.pdf.

149. Jon Burnett et al., ''State-sponsored cruelty': Children in immigration detention', Medical Justice, March 2016, http://www.medicaljustice.org.uk/wp-content/uploads/2016/03/state-sponsored-cruelty.pdf.

150. Phil Miller, 'Britain's Loneliest Migrant Centre Is an Isolated Hell for its Detainees', *Vice*, 13 January 2016, https://www.vice.com/en_uk/article/the-verne-britains-lonliest-migrant-detention-centren-923.

151. UNHCR, 'Ending statelessness within 10 years', http://www.unhcr.org/546217229.pdf.

152. Bobbie Mills, 'Citizenship deprivation: How Britain took the lead on dismantling citizenship', European Network on Statelessness, 3 March 2016, http://www.statelessness.eu/blog/citizenship-deprivation-how-britain-took-lead-dismantling-citizenship.

153. Victoria Parsons, 'Theresa May deprived 33 individuals of British citizenship in 2015', Bureau of Investigative Journalism, 21 June 2016, https://www.thebureauinvestigates.com/stories/2016-06-21/citizenship-stripping-new-figures-reveal-theresa-may-has-deprived-33-individuals-of-british-citizenship.

154. Alice Ross and Patrick Galey, 'Home Secretary pushes through 'controversial' powers to make people stateless', Bureau of Investigative Journalism, 30 January 2014, https://www.thebureauinvestigates.com/stories/2014-01-30/home-secretary-pushes-through-controversial-powers-to-make-people-stateless.

155. David Anderson QC, 'Citizenship removal resulting in statelessness', April 2016, https://www.gov.uk/government/uploads/system/uploads/attachment_data/file/518120/David_

Anderson_QC_-_CITIZENSHIP_REMOVAL__web_.pdf.

156. Louis Reynolds, 'Statelessness isn't a solution', Demos, https://www.demos.co.uk/blog/statelessness-isnt-a-solution/.

157. Laura Hughes, 'Syrian president's British-born wife Asma al-Assad faces calls to be stripped of her UK citizenship', *Telegraph*, 16 April 2017, http://www.telegraph.co.uk/news/2017/04/16/syrian-presidents-british-born-wife-asma-al-assad-faces-calls/.

158. BBC, 'Government rejects pardon request for Alan Turing', 8 March 2012, http://www.bbc.co.uk/news/technology-16919012.

159. BBC, 'Royal pardon for codebreaker Alan Turing', 24 December 2013, http://www.bbc.co.uk/news/technology-25495315.

160. Raziye Akkoc, 'Mapped: Where is same sex marriage legal in the world?', *Telegraph*, 21 May 2015, http://www.telegraph.co.uk/news/worldnews/europe/ireland/11621812/Mapped-Where-is-same-sex-marriage-legal-in-the-world.html.

161. George Eaton, 'Blow for Cameron as 128 Tory MPs vote against gay marriage', *New Statesman*, 21 May 2013, http://www.newstatesman.com/politics/2013/05/blow-cameron-128-tory-mps-vote-against-gay-marriage. BBC News Online, 'MP-by-MP: Gay marriage vote', 5 February 2013, http://www.bbc.co.uk/news/uk-politics-21346694.

162. BBC, ''Turing Bill' for gay pardons fails in Parliament', 21 October 2016, http://www.bbc.co.uk/news/uk-politics-37707030.

163. Ministry of Justice and Sam Gyimah, 'Thousands officially pardoned under "Turing's Law"', HMG, 31 January 2017, https://www.gov.uk/government/news/thousands-officially-pardoned-under-turings-law.

164. HMG Department for Communities and Local Government, 'English Housing Survey: Headline Report 2014-15', https://www.gov.uk/government/uploads/system/uploads/attachment_data/file/501065/EHS_Headline_report_2014-15.pdf. Shelter, 'Three quarters of Britons fear future generations will

never have a 'forever home'', 21 March 2016, https://england.shelter.org.uk/media/press_releases/articles/three_quarters_of_britons_fear_future_generations_will_never_have_a_forever_home.

165. HMG Treasury, 'UK Housing Market Trends', http://pricedout.org.uk/Download/Treasury_PM_Housing_Brief_FOI_release.pdf.

166. In the same place.

167. In the same place.

168. ONS, 'Housing affordability in England and Wales: 1997 to 2016', https://www.ons.gov.uk/peoplepopulationandcommunity/housing/bulletins/housingaffordabilityinenglandandwales/1997to2016#effect-of-workplace-based-and-residence-based-earnings-on-housing-affordability. Gavin Jackson, 'UK house prices "least affordable ever"', *FT*, 17 March 2017, www.ft.com/content/ea8f28fc-0b08-11e7-ac5a-903b21361b43+&cd=1&hl=en&ct=clnk&gl=uk.

169. Larry Elliott, 'Generation rent', *Guardian*, 27 December 2016, https://www.theguardian.com/society/2016/dec/27/home-ownership-figures-are-exaggerated-says-thinktank-resolution-foundation.

170. Dan Wilson Craw, 'Renters at higher risk of mental health problems', Generation Rent, 26 February 2015, http://www.generationrent.org/renters_at_higher_risk_of_mental_health_problems.

171. Sarah Knapton, 'Soaring house prices reduce number of babies born in England', *Telegraph*, 12 April 2017, http://www.telegraph.co.uk/science/2017/04/12/soaring-house-prices-reduce-number-babies-born-england/. 24 Housing, 'Renting 'lifers' £500,000 worse off than those who buy in their 20s', 25 March 2015, http://www.24housing.co.uk/yournews/renting-lifers-500000-worse-off-than-those-who-buy-in-their-20s/.

172. HMG, Communications Act 2003, http://www.legislation.gov.

uk/ukpga/2003/21/pdfs/ukpga_20030021_en.pdf.

173. Gareth Corfield, 'Arrests for 'offensive' Twitter and Facebook messages up by a third', *The Register*, 2 June 2016, http://www.theregister.co.uk/2016/06/02/social_media_arrests_up_37pc_london_section_127_communications_act/.

174. Helen Carter, 'Man gets community sentence for Facebook post about dead soldiers', *Guardian*, 9 October 2012, https://www.theguardian.com/uk/2012/oct/09/community-sentence-facebook-dead-soldiers.

175. In the same place.

176. Richard Seymour, 'Azhar Ahmed – charged with treason over Facebook comments?', *Guardian*, 15 March 2012, https://www.theguardian.com/commentisfree/libertycentral/2012/mar/15/azhar-ahmed-treason-army-facebook-comments.

177. Niamh O'Doherty, '"I'm so sorry": The moment shamed teenager who posted Facebook picture of burning poppy on Remembrance Sunday was forced to make humbling apology to war widows and veterans', *Daily Mail*, 20 December 2012, http://www.dailymail.co.uk/news/article-2251196/Moment-Linford-House-posted-Facebook-picture-burning-poppy-forced-apologise-widows-veterans.html.

178. Richard Spillett, '"I'm glad that teacher got stabbed up': Facebook troll who wrote disgusting messages after Ann Maguire was killed in her classroom is jailed', *Daily Mail*, 4 June 2014, http://www.dailymail.co.uk/news/article-2648421/Im-glad-teacher-got-stabbed-Facebook-troll-wrote-disgusting-messages-Ann-Maguire-killed-classroom-jailed.html.

179. Jocelyn Y. Stewart, 'UC scholar studied Upper Nile Valley', *LA Times*, 25 April 2008, http://articles.latimes.com/2008/apr/25/local/me-collins25.

180. Adam Cohen, '"Libel Tourism': When Freedom of Speech Takes a Holiday', *NYT*, 14 September 2008, http://www.nytimes.com/2008/09/15/opinion/15mon4.html. Duncan Campbell, 'British libel laws violate human rights, says UN', *Guard-*

ian, 14 August 2008, https://www.theguardian.com/uk/2008/aug/14/law.unitednations.

181. HMG Defamation Act 2013, http://www.legislation.gov.uk/ukpga/2013/26/pdfs/ukpga_20130026_en.pdf.

182. Matthew Taylor, Nick Hopkins and Phil Maynard, 'UK's reputation is damaged by reaction to Edward Snowden, says UN official', *Guardian*, 15 November 2013, https://www.theguardian.com/world/2013/nov/15/uk-reputation-edward-snowden-un.

183. See my *Britain's Secret Wars*, 2016, Clairview Books.

184. BBC, 'UK regulator revokes Kurdish Med TV's licence', 23 April 1999, http://news.bbc.co.uk/1/hi/world/monitoring/326883.stm.

185. *Britain's Secret Wars*, in the work cited.

186. David Blair, 'Britain bans Iran's Press TV from airwaves', *Telegraph*, 20 January 2012, http://www.telegraph.co.uk/news/worldnews/middleeast/iran/9028435/Britain-bans-Irans-Press-TV-from-airwaves.html.

187. *Britain's Secret Wars*, in the work cited.

188. HMG, Serious Organised Crime and Police Act 2005, http://www.legislation.gov.uk/ukpga/2005/15/contents.

189. HMG, Police Reform and Social Responsibility Act 2011, www.legislation.gov.uk/ukpga/2011/13/contents/enacted.

190. Liberty and NUS, 'Protest: Your Rights', 2009, https://www.liberty-human-rights.org.uk/sites/default/files/nusliberty-rights-document-a5.pdf.

191. Paul Lewis and Rob Evans, 2013, *Undercover*, Faber and Faber.

192. NETCU, http://netcu.org.uk/.

193. Vikram Dodd and Paul Lewis, 'Kettling of G20 protesters by police was illegal, high court rules', *Guardian*, 14 April 2011, https://www.theguardian.com/uk/2011/apr/14/kettling-g20-protesters-police-illegal.

194. UN Office of the High Commissioner for Human Rights, 'Statement by the United Nations Special Rapporteur on the

rights to freedom of peaceful assembly and of association at the conclusion of his visit to the United Kingdom', 23 January 2013, https://web.archive.org/web/20130905105909/http://www.ohchr.org/EN/NewsEvents/Pages/DisplayNews.aspx-?NewsID=12945&LangID=E.

195. Royals, 'The role of Monarchy', https://www.royal.uk/role-monarchy. Royals, 'Coronation Oath, 1953', 2 June 1953, https://www.royal.uk/coronation-oath-2-june-1953.   Parliament, 'Lords Spiritual and Temporal', http://www.parliament.uk/site-information/glossary/lords-spiritual-and-temporal/.

196. City of London Corporation, 'The City's government', https://www.cityoflondon.gov.uk/about-the-city/history/Pages/city-government.aspx.

197. BBC, 'Election 2017: The result in maps and charts', 10 June 2017, http://www.bbc.co.uk/news/election-2017-40176349.

198. BBC, 'Election 2017: Results', http://www.bbc.co.uk/news/election/2017/results.

199. Louis Doré, 'Here's what the UK electoral map would look like with Proportional Representation', *Independent*, no date, https://www.indy100.com/article/uk-election-map-proportional-representation-system-2017-conservative-labour-7784956.

200. *Science Daily*, 'Denmark, Finland and Belgium have best democracies, experts say', 27 January 2011, https://www.sciencedaily.com/releases/2011/01/110127090533.htm.

201. Ipsos-Mori, 'Veracity Index 2015', January 2016, https://www.ipsos.com/sites/default/files/migrations/en-uk/files/Assets/Docs/Polls/ipsos-mori-veracity-index-2015-charts.pdf.

202. Peter Kellner, 'Democracy on trial', YouGov and Reuters Institute for the Study of Journalism, March 2012, http://cdn.yougov.com/cumulus_uploads/document/ww4o7wko1q/WebVersion_Democracy%20in%20Britain%20A5.pdf.

203. In the same place.

204. Andrew Grice, 'Majority of British voters agree with Corbyn's

claim UK foreign policy increases risk of terrorism', *Independent*, 6 June 2017, http://www.independent.co.uk/news/uk/politics/jeremy-corbyn-poll-foreign-policy-terrorism-british-voters-agree-majority-latest-a7776276.html.

205. Matthew Smith, 'Nationalisation vs privatisation: the public view', YouGov, 19 May 2017, https://yougov.co.uk/news/2017/05/19/nationalisation-vs-privatisation-public-view/.

206. Patrick Butler, 'Thousands have died after being found fit for work, DWP figures show', *Guardian*, 27 August 2015, https://www.theguardian.com/society/2015/aug/27/thousands-died-after-fit-for-work-assessment-dwp-figures.

207. Alan Markey, 'UN condemns UK benefit sanctions regime', NAWRA, 14 July 2016, http://www.nawra.org.uk/index.php/un-condemns-uk-benefit-sanctions-regime/.

208. Anthony Wells, 'Strong public support for benefit cuts', YouGov, 16 May 2011, https://yougov.co.uk/news/2011/05/16/strong-public-support-benefit-cuts/.

209. Strathclyde University, Glasgow University Media Group and Inclusion London, 'Bad News for Disabled People: How the newspapers are reporting disability', http://www.gla.ac.uk/media/media_214917_en.pdf.

210. Andrew Hood and Agnes Norris Keiller, 'A survey of the UK benefit system', Institute for Fiscal Studies, BN13, November 2016, https://www.ifs.org.uk/bns/bn13.pdf. DWP, 'Fraud and Error in the Benefit System 2013/14 Estimates (biannual)', https://www.gov.uk/government/uploads/system/uploads/attachment_data/file/371459/Statistical_Release.pdf.

211. In the same place and Church of England, 'Guide to Welfare Reforms: 2010-2017', Annex 1, https://www.churchofengland.org/media/1783349/gs%201897%20-%20annex%201.pdf.

212. In the same place.

213. In the same place.

214. In the same place.

215. In the same place.

216. In the same place.

217. Ian Dunt, 'The myth of welfare tourism: European body find UK benefits "manifestly inadequate"', *Politics*, 30 January 2014, www.politics.co.uk/news/2014/01/30/the-myth-of-welfare-tourism-european-body-find-uk-benefits-m+&c-d=9&hl=en&ct=clnk&gl=uk.

218. Church of England, in the work cited.

219. ILO, 'Ratifications for United Kingdom', http://www.ilo.org/dyn/normlex/en/f?p=1000:11200:0::NO:11200:P11200_COUNTRY_ID:102651.

220. Chris Syder, 'Striking out', *New Law Journal*, 15 July 2015, https://www.newlawjournal.co.uk/content/striking-out-0.

221. Bart Cammaerts, 'Zero-hours contracts: a post-modern form of slavery which faces little real opposition from the unions', LSE, 27 February 2015, http://blogs.lse.ac.uk/politicsandpolicy/zero-hours-contracts-a-post-modern-form-of-slavery-which-faces-little-real-opposition-from-the-unions/.

222. Shiv Malik and James Ball, 'More jobseekers told to do unpaid work or face possible loss of benefits', *Guardian*, 12 June 2012, https://www.theguardian.com/society/2012/jun/12/jobseekers-work-unpaid-lose-benefits. FOIA request, 'Names of placement providers...', https://www.whatdotheyknow.com/request/348484/response/845583/attach/3/326%202012%20Info.pdf.

223. Aidan McQuade interviewed by Press TV, 'Slave Labour UK', 6 September 2014, https://www.youtube.com/watch?v=-bclu-9aPCGs.

224. OECD, 'Key Issues for Labour Market and Social Policies', https://www.oecd.org/els/emp/4358365.pdf. Andy Charlwood, 'The Anatomy of Union Decline in Britain 1990-1998', LSE, December 2003, http://eprints.lse.ac.uk/20006/1/The_Anatomy_of_Union_Decline_in_Britain_1990-1998.pdf.

225. Institute of Employment Rights, 'United Nations criticises

UK's "undue constraints" on trade union rights', 1 February 2013, http://www.ier.org.uk/news/united-nations-criticises-uks-undue-constraints-trade-union-rights.

226. John Hendy, 'More anti-union legislation in the UK', *International Union Rights*, 2015, 22(2): 22-3.

227. Mercer, 'UK receives second lowest public holiday entitlement in the world', 9 September 2014, https://www.mercer.com/newsroom/public-holiday-entitlements.html.

228. *Guardian*, 'Who works the longest hours in Europe?', Datablog, 8 December 2011, https://www.theguardian.com/news/datablog/2011/dec/08/europe-working-hours.

229. Glassdoor, 'Where Are The Best Social Benefits In Europe? It Certainly Isn't Britain', 18 February 2016, https://www.glassdoor.co.uk/blog/social-benefits-europe-isnt-britain/.   TUC, 'UK in the relegation zone for decently-paid maternity leave in Europe, warns TUC', March 2017, https://www.tuc.org.uk/equality-issues/gender-equality/pregnancy-discrimination/uk-relegation-zone-decently-paid-maternity.

230. BBC Magazine, 'Are lunch breaks really for wimps?', 1 August 2008, http://news.bbc.co.uk/1/hi/magazine/7549300.stm. Adam Gale, 'Most workers are missing lunch, according to a new survey. But is it really bad for productivity? Put down your sandwich and find out', *Management Today*, 18 February 2015, www.managementtoday.co.uk/lets-not-lunch-skipping-breaks-reducing-british-productivity/article/1328066+&cd=5&hl=en&ct=clnk&gl=uk.

231. Hilary Osborne, 'UK workers "unhappiest in Europe"', *Guardian*, 7 June 2005, https://www.theguardian.com/money/2005/jun/07/workandcareers.business. ACAS, 'Can't get no satisfaction: UK workers among the most dissatisfied in Europe', 2012, http://www.acas.org.uk/index.aspx?articleid=3924.

232. NatCen, www.bsa.natcen.ac.uk.

233. Serina Sandhu, 'Working makes British people unhappy, new study finds', *Independent*, 3 February 2016, http://www.inde-

pendent.co.uk/news/uk/home-news/working-makes-british-people-unhappy-new-study-finds-a6850766.html.

234. Roz Sanderson, 'How happy are UK workers compared to those in Europe?', *Safety and Health Practitioner*, 10 March 2017, https://www.shponline.co.uk/50008-2/.

235. Gordon Brown, 'Promises, promises: what Gordon Brown said', *Guardian*, 18 February 2009, https://www.theguardian.com/politics/2009/feb/18/ending-child-poverty-brown.

236. ITV, 'UK among 'worst rates of stillbirth in western Europe'', 30 June 2014, http://www.itv.com/news/story/2014-06-30/still-birth-among-worst-in-western-europe/.

237. The study was updated in 2017 and revealed '(a)n alarming gap between rich and poor', putting the UK 15 out of 19 for infant deaths in Western countries. Louise Prime, 'UK child health near bottom in Europe', OnMedica, 26 January 2017, http://www.onmedica.com/newsArticle.aspx?id=52ba40b6-0914-411d-aaa4-29c75ad7bd59.

238. Paul Gregg, Susan Harkness and Stephen Machin, 'Poor Kids: Trends in Child Poverty in Britain, 1968–96', *Fiscal Studies* (1999), 20(2): 163-187

239. John Micklewright and Kitty Stewart (UNICEF), 'Child well-being and social cohesion: Is the UK the oddball in Europe?', *New Economy*, 2000, 18-23, http://www.blackwellpublishing.com/content/BPL_Images/Journal_Samples/NEWE1070-3535~7~1/115.PDF. Lucy Ward, 'Britain bottom of table for child well-being', *Guardian*, 17 March 2000, https://www.theguardian.com/uk/2000/mar/17/lucyward.

240. UNICEF, 'Child poverty in perspective', Report Card 7, 2007, https://www.unicef-irc.org/publications/pdf/rc7_eng.pdf.

241. In the same place.

242. In the same place.

243. In the same place.

244. Lucy Ward, 'Mother of truant sent back to prison', *Guardian*, 24 March 2004, https://www.theguardian.com/uk/2004/

mar/24/schools.education.

245. In the same place.

246. Graeme Paton, 'School is boring and irrelevant, say teenagers', *Telegraph*, 21 January 2009, http://www.telegraph.co.uk/education/secondaryeducation/4297452/School-is-boring-and-irrelevant-say-teenagers.html. David Rhodes, 'Number of children taught in large classes trebles', BBC News Online, 10 January 2017, http://www.bbc.co.uk/news/uk-england-38506305.

247. Sally Weale, 'English children among the unhappiest in the world at school due to bullying', *Guardian*, 19 August 2015, https://www.theguardian.com/society/2015/aug/19/english-children-among-unhappiest-world-widespread-bullying.

248. Judith Burns, 'Primary pupils 'feel test pressure', survey', BBC News Online, 9 May 2016, http://www.bbc.co.uk/news/education-36229995.

249. Press Association, 'More parents in England prosecuted for taking children out of school', 12 August 2015, https://www.theguardian.com/education/2015/aug/12/increase-parents-england-prosecuted-taking-children-out-of-school.

250. Warwick Mansell and Patrick Edwards, 'DIY schooling on the rise as more parents opt for home education', *Guardian*, 12 April 2016, https://www.theguardian.com/education/2016/apr/12/home-schooling-parents-education-children-england.

251. Hannah Ellis-Petersen, 'Middle class people dominate arts, survey finds', *Guardian*, 23 November 2015, https://www.theguardian.com/artanddesign/2015/nov/23/middle-class-people-dominate-arts-survey-finds.

252. Mark Easton, 'Is Britain's class gap finally starting to narrow?', BBC, 9 June 2016, http://www.bbc.co.uk/news/explainers-36488032.

253. Richard Russell, 'All our children', Arts Council England, 13 January 2017, http://www.artscouncil.org.uk/blog/all-our-children.

254. Elizabeth Gibney, 'United Kingdom: The paths not taken', *Nature* (Is science only for the rich?), 21 September 2016, http://www.nature.com/news/is-science-only-for-the-rich-1.20650#UK.

255. Lib Dems, Manifesto 2017, http://d3n8a8pro7vhmx.cloudfront.net/themes/5909d4366ad575794c000000/attachments/original/1495020157/Manifesto-Final.pdf?1495020157. For the Cable quotes and context, see my *Britain's Secret Wars*, 2016, Clairview Books.

256. National Archives (UK), 'Getting the vote: Voting rights before 1832', no date, http://www.nationalarchives.gov.uk/pathways/citizenship/struggle_democracy/getting_vote.htm.

257. Nigel Lawson, 'The New Conservatism', 4 August 1980, Bow Group, http://fc95d419f4478b3b6e5f3f71d0fe2b653c4f-00f32175760e96e7.r87.cf1.rackcdn.com/800804%20The%20New%20Conservatism%20f77.pdf.

258. Margaret Thatcher Foundation, 'Interview for Woman's Own ("no such thing as society")', 23 September 1987, http://www.margaretthatcher.org/document/106689.

259. Barclays, 'UK prosperity map', https://wealth.barclays.com/en_gb/home/research/research-centre/uk-wealth-prosperity-map.html.

260. Bernado's, 'Child poverty statistics and facts', https://www.barnardos.org.uk/what_we_do/our_work/child_poverty/child_poverty_what_is_poverty/child_poverty_statistics_facts.htm. Graham Whitham, 'Inequality and division in the UK', Oxfam, 13 September 2016, http://policy-practice.oxfam.org.uk/blog/2016/09/inequality-and-division-in-the-uk--ensuring-the-economy-works-for-everyone. RCPCH, 'Poverty and child health: views from the frontline' (Summary), May 2017, https://spark.adobe.com/page/so9bu5k2Fjs6f/.

261. Michael Savage, 'May school lunch cut 'would hit 900,000 children of struggling families'', *Guardian*, 20 May 2017, https://www.theguardian.com/politics/2017/may/20/theresa-may-

school-meals-plan-hits-900000-families.

262. Social Mobility Commission, 2016, https://www.gov.uk/
government/uploads/system/uploads/attachment_data/
file/569410/Social_Mobility_Commission_2016_REPORT_
WEB__1__.pdf. *Independent*, 'Over 50,000 families shipped out
of London boroughs in the past three years due to welfare cuts
and soaring rents', 29 April 2015, http://www.independent.
co.uk/news/uk/home-news/over-50000-families-shipped-out-
of-london-in-the-past-three-years-due-to-welfare-cuts-and-
soaring-10213854.html.

263. Social Mobility, in the work cited.

264. BBC, 'Pensioners' life expectancy falls back', 29 March 2017,
http://www.bbc.co.uk/news/business-39429039.

Index

About the author

T.J. Coles received his PhD from the University of Plymouth, UK, in 2017 for work on the aesthetic experiences of blind and visually impaired people. His research draws on the philosophy of cognitive psychology and neuroscience.

A columnist with *Axis of Logic*, Coles's political works include *Britain's Secret Wars*, *The Great Brexit Swindle*, *President Trump, Inc.* and the anthology *Voices for Peace* which he edited (all Clairview Books).

BOOKS

Iff Books

ACADEMIC AND SPECIALIST

Iff Books publishes non-fiction. It aims to work with authors and titles that augment our understanding of the human condition, society and civilisation, and the world or universe in which we live.
If you have enjoyed this book, why not tell other readers by posting a review on your preferred book site.
Recent bestsellers from Iff Books are:

Why Materialism Is Baloney
How True Skeptics Know There is no Death and Fathom Answers to Life, the Universe, and Everything
Bernardo Kastrup
A hard-nosed, logical, and skeptic non-materialist metaphysics, according to which the body is in mind, not mind in the body.
Paperback: 978-1-78279-362-5 ebook: 978-1-78279-361-8

The Fall
Steve Taylor
The Fall discusses human achievement versus the issues of war, patriarchy and social inequality.
Paperback: 978-1-90504-720-8 ebook: 978-184694-633-2

Brief Peeks Beyond
Critical Essays on Metaphysics, Neuroscience, Free Will,
Skepticism and Culture
Bernardo Kastrup
An incisive, original, compelling alternative to current mainstream
cultural views and assumptions.
Paperback: 978-1-78535-018-4 ebook: 978-1-78535-019-1

Framespotting
Changing How You Look at Things Changes How
You See Them
Laurence & Alison Matthews
A punchy, upbeat guide to framespotting. Spot deceptions and
hidden assumptions; swap growth for growing up. See and be free.
Paperback: 978-1-78279-689-3 ebook: 978-1-78279-822-4

Is There an Afterlife?
David Fontana
Is there an Afterlife? If so what is it like? How do Western ideas
of the afterlife compare with Eastern? David Fontana presents
the historical and contemporary evidence for survival of physical
death.
Paperback: 978-1-90381-690-5

Nothing Matters
A Book About Nothing
Ronald Green
Thinking about Nothing opens the world to everything by
illuminating new angles to old problems and stimulating new
ways of thinking.
Paperback: 978-1-84694-707-0 ebook: 978-1-78099-016-3

Panpsychism

The Philosophy of the Sensuous Cosmos

Peter Ells

Are free will and mind chimeras? This book, anti-materialistic but respecting science, answers: No! Mind is foundational to all existence.

Paperback: 978-1-84694-505-2 ebook: 978-1-78099-018-7

Punk Science

Inside the Mind of God

Manjir Samanta-Laughton

Many have experienced unexplainable phenomena; God, psychic abilities, extraordinary healing and angelic encounters. Can cutting-edge science actually explain phenomena previously thought of as 'paranormal'?

Paperback: 978-1-90504-793-2

The Vagabond Spirit of Poetry

Edward Clarke

Spend time with the wisest poets of the modern age and of the past, and let Edward Clarke remind you of the importance of poetry in our industrialized world.

Paperback: 978-1-78279-370-0 ebook: 978-1-78279-369-4

Readers of ebooks can buy or view any of these bestsellers by clicking on the live link in the title. Most titles are published in paperback and as an ebook. Paperbacks are available in traditional bookshops. Both print and ebook formats are available online. Find more titles and sign up to our readers' newsletter at http://www.johnhuntpublishing.com/non-fiction Follow us on Facebook at https://www.facebook.com/JHPNonFiction and Twitter at https://twitter.com/JHPNonFiction